7/14/06

1314
BANNOCKBURN

1314

BANNOCKBURN

TEMPUS

Cover illustration: Brass of Robert Bruce, Dunfermline Abbey, courtesy of
Campbell McCutcheon.

Tempus Publishing Limited
The Mill, Brimscombe Port,
Stroud, Gloucestershire, GL5 2QG

ISBN 0 7524 2982 5

Typesetting and origination by Tempus Publishing Limited

Contents

About the Author

Aryeh Nusbacher is Senior Lecturer in War Studies at the Royal Military Academy, Sandhurst. He was the historical consultant for a recent History Channel/Discovery Channel television documentary on Bannockburn and currently co-presents BBC2's *Time Commanders*. His next book, *Blood on the Strand: London's Civil War*, will be published by Tempus.

Acknowledgements

Thanks to Miriam Nusbacher for her criticism and to Paul McCann for the same; to Janice Liedl, Rosemary Beasley, Cliveden Chew Haas and Barry Sloan for their technical advice; to Mike Myatt and Jeremy Graham for their services as sounding boards; to Jeff Singman and Janice Liedl for translations and to Joseph Goering who got me angry enough to write this book.

The author and publishers would like to acknowledge the following picture sources: illustrations 28 and 33, the collection of Bob McCutcheon; colour plates 35-39 and 46-48, © Cromwell Productions Ltd; colour plates 40-45, © The Bruce Pictures Ltd; colour plates 49 and 50, original image © Cromwell Productions Ltd, additions by the author. The sketches numbered 51, 52, 64, 71, 72 and 77 are by the author. All other illustrations are from the Tempus Archive.

Preface: The Ladies in the Cages

I lie in this cage,
In full public gaze,
But I don't give a pin for all their scorn,
For I've crowned my love a king,
Ah! Such glorious days I've seen.
Give me the chance, I'd do it all again.

'Isabel', traditional song

Isabel, Countess of Buchan, lived like an animal in a wooden
cage but she was lucky to be alive. After the betrayal and fall
of Kildrummy Castle in 1306, the English king had taken ter-
rible vengeance on the defenders. Young Sir Nigel Bruce,
who had commanded the garrison to great effect and had
nearly driven the English away from its walls, was dragged
through the streets of Berwick on a hurdle, hanged, then cut
down while still alive and beheaded; the other captured
defenders suffered the same fate. Even the blacksmith who
had betrayed the castle by setting its stores of grain on fire was
killed, his golden reward poured molten down his throat. The
Earl of Atholl had taken the ladies in the castle to sanctuary
at St Duthac's Abbey, whence they were dragged by King

Edward's men. Atholl was allowed to ride a horse to his execution in England, and hanged from especially high gallows before being beheaded and having his head impaled on an especially high spike on London Bridge. He was, after all, an earl.

The ladies had been allowed to live. Queen Elizabeth of Scotland, daughter of the powerful English Earl of Ulster, was fortunate enough to be locked up with elderly and dull ladies-in-waiting. Christina Bruce, her sister-in-law, was sent to a nunnery. For Isabel of Buchan, Mary Bruce (the Scottish king's sister), and Queen Elizabeth's daughter Marjorie, King Edward had a less pleasant fate. He ordered cages to be built on the walls of Berwick and Roxburgh castles, and of the Tower of London.

Isabel was locked in the cage in Berwick, Mary in Roxburgh and young Marjorie, twelve years old, was locked in the cage in London. There they were exposed to the jeers and abuse of the townsfolk, and their only privacy lay in the privies built within the walls, in deference to their sex. They spoke with nobody except their maids, and the little girl was forbidden to speak with anyone apart from the constable of the Tower.

The youngest was sent to a nunnery after a short while, but Isabel and Mary spent four years caged on the castle walls like beasts in a menagerie, living monuments to King Edward Longshanks's burning anger against the Earl of Carrick who had betrayed him.

Introduction

On Midsummer's Day, 1314, two groups of men met near Stirling Castle, and many people died. That is the truth.

It is difficult to determine just what the word 'truth' means, never mind the true story of one day's fighting in Scotland several hundred years ago. Philosophers do a good trade in discussing the meaning of truth, and I don't mean to take business away from them. So, having described the truth of the matter at the top of the page, the rest of this book will leave the issue of truth alone and attempt merely to describe, as factually as possible, the events of the day based on what sources we have.

We have no eyewitness accounts of the Battle of Bannockburn. There is little of what an historian calls 'primary source material'. There are second-hand accounts, there are inferences we can make and there are authorities we can consult, but we have no direct description by an observer. It is not necessarily true that this lack is an insurmountable handicap. Police scientists tell us that the account of an eye-witness, no matter how well-meaning, is notoriously unreliable. Thus we might even look upon our lack of an eyewitness account as an advantage.

This is not to say that we cannot describe accurately the events which occurred at Stirling on 24 June 1314. A detective can investigate a crime, whether he has a witness or not. Just so, we can piece together the motives, the opportunities and the weapons that resulted in the violence of Bannockburn. Like the detective I will describe something I have not seen, but which I infer and deduce. Like a detective giving evidence to a jury, I will describe the events as though I were speaking the truth. I will occasionally put likely words in the mouths of the participants. Like that jury you must view my inferences sceptically, and you may choose to believe me or not.

We have a few informants to work with in our investigation. One is Sir Thomas Gray of Heton, whose father (Thomas senior) fought at Bannockburn and was captured. Another is Master John Barbour, Archdeacon of Aberdeen, who worshipped Robert the Bruce as though the Scots king had been a voting member of the Holy Trinity. Barbour's account, from some fifty years after the incident, is written from hearsay. His language is flowery court Scots, the English dialect that was the vernacular and literary language of the Scottish Lowlands.

The anonymous author of the Lanercost Chronicle pitches in, writing from the point of view of an English monastic community near the Scottish border. We also have documentary evidence provided by the English king himself. All the correspondence of the English kings was recorded in chancery rolls; the medieval equivalent of the modern office's day-book. Useful information comes to us from the Patent Rolls and the Fine Rolls. File copies of correspondence were kept in other rolls, such as the Scottish Rolls, which contain all the English royal correspondence regarding Scottish affairs.

The unknown illuminator of the Luttrell Psalter has given us many pictures of English knights, archers and common folk, going about their trades in the sort of normalcy that lets us guess that they are an actual depiction of daily life some twenty years after the fighting at Bannockburn. The illuminator has included some very fine detail, including such mundane articles as shoe-straps and horseshoe cleats, that sometimes tell us more in one square inch of illustration than Archdeacon Barbour tells us in pages of text.

Military historians traditionally approach a battle from its conclusion. They start by deciding who won the battle, and then work backwards to decide why one side won and the other side lost. This methodology comes from the fact that the primary employment of military historians in the past has been at war colleges, staff colleges and military academies; places where the focus of military history is to teach students how to repeat the successes and avoid the mistakes of their professional predecessors. This school of history has told us whom to blame for countless defeats, and whom to worship for countless victories, and as long as you are a tactician or strategist looking for professional guidance, or a military buff looking for conversational pointers, this school provides adequate history. This is, however, a simplistic approach in that it is so oriented towards the final outcome of the battle that it ignores every single aspect of warfare that does not contribute directly to the victory of the victor or the defeat of the defeated.

I propose to walk around to the other side of the battle, and begin before the beginning. I've taken all the evidence available to me, and tried to sift it without regard to victory, blame or traditional military history. I plan to take the reader through the process that resulted in vast expenditure of money and human life over the course of a year. At the other end of the battle, and at the other end of the book, the reader will understand a great deal about what happened near the shores of the Bannockburn. This account does not agree completely with any modern or medieval account of the battle – for one reason or another, every previous account of the battle is in some way incomplete. I do not claim to be entirely right, I merely claim that this description of the Battle of Bannockburn is less wrong than previous descriptions.

Some lengthy discussion of the site of the battle will be necessary in the course of my arguments. This is important because the characteristics of the ground under the soldiers' feet were the most important influence on the outcome of the battle. Had the most important battle of 1314 been fought in some other part of Stirlingshire, or in nearby Peebles, the story would likely have been very different indeed. The argument on the *locus in quo* will be lengthy because it is complicated, and in order for the author as detective to make the case to the reader as the jury, he must explain in detail.

Previous accounts of the battle fall into three categories. One is the medieval account, written by people like Thomas Gray and John Barbour. The next is the military account, often written by a retired army officer, which seeks to fit Bannockburn into the modern military frame of reference. The third is the modern historian who believes the accounts of the above two categories. None of these people is a villain or a dupe. All put pen to paper with the best of motives, and the result is a morass of myth, unlikely guesswork and *Sturm und Drang* thundering which prevents the modern reader from understanding what really happened.

The medieval chroniclers of Bannockburn were all in some way interested parties. The monks at Lanercost were unimpressed with King Edward, and still less impressed with the prospect of paying blackmail to Bruce and his *famiglia* of Norman-Scottish gangsters. Thomas Gray heard the story from his father, who was captured during the battle (and therefore had to be ransomed back from the Scots) and thus we have an English partisan who might have been a bit disgruntled with the conduct of the campaign. Barbour, on the other hand, was a poet interested in memorialising Robert Bruce as an epic hero with all the valour and holiness of a warrior-prophet.

The military writers tended to view Bannockburn through a filter of Napoleonic training and tactics. They see the armies as ciphers on a map, which manoeuvre in wheels and countermarches, with a front line between them, fighting a battle with a beginning, a middle and an end. They have Victorian medievalist illusions about the conduct of a medieval battle. They tend to treat it as though it were a chivalric exercise between knights rather than a few thousand men who wanted to live to go home and were perfectly willing to put the boot in to further that end.

The conduct of the battle is not the only fertile ground for illusion. The composition of the armies, for example, is subject to modern notions. Every Scots lad who hears tales of Bannockburn from his grandfather or from a boy's book on the subject must have visions of a Scottish army of kilted and bonneted lads marching to the pipes and shouting 'Claymore!' The English side is populated by heavily armoured men with Oxbridge accents and heraldic surcoats, accompanied by a peppering of renegade Scots who twirl their traitorous moustaches. At work here is the modern view of the state, and the state's army. The modern assumption is that if the king of England went to war against the king of Scotland he took with him an English army to fight a Scottish army. The reality was that Scotland was a feuding collection of patriarchal tribes and jealous barons rather than anything resembling a modern state. The reality for the English was that a medieval king was the man perched precariously atop a feudal pyramid rather than the ruler of a nation. It was this pair of realities, that of a divided nation of Scots facing a feudal king of the English, that shaped Bannockburn. Imposing modern ideas of England and Scotland, treason and chivalry, over the realities that applied in June of 1314 obscures the real story of the battle.

The legends of Bannockburn also do a good job of obscuring the reality of the battle and the personalities involved. The Anglo-Norman baron Robert de Brus is hardly the common conception of the bold king of Scots. Centuries of myth and strong modern and ethnic preconceptions combine to give us the picture of a Rabby Bruce, who on his deathbed whispered, 'tak' ma heart tae the Holy Land,' in a Glasgow accent. Likewise the character of Edward II has been misrepresented through legend, suffering from unfavourable comparison to his father and his son. Allegations of homosexuality produce a view of an effeminate coward and cuckold, dandling his favourites on the royal knee and becoming petulant when his pets were attacked.

The Battle of Bannockburn carries a great deal of mythological baggage as battles go. No other battle in the wars of Scottish independence is either as eulogised or as misconceived as Bannockburn. Indeed, with the exception of Flodden and Culloden, no Scottish battle is as prominent in the history and legendry of Britain. This is not because

Bannockburn was of itself an especially significant battle. The student of history who looks for the rise of a Scottish commonwealth after 1314 will see a bleak prospect indeed. After this battle, Robert Bruce established no Scots kingdom, but continued his guerrilla campaign of raiding, punctuated by occasional miserable failure in a pitched battle, for the rest of his life. The military might of England can scarcely be said to have been affected by the battle, since in that summer of 1314 the military classes of England stayed away from Stirling in droves. Nor can the prestige of the English king be said to have been demolished there, since Edward II went north with little prestige that spring, and his prestige fell off only slowly (though surely) through the rest of his reign and after two more Scottish campaigns.

Bannockburn is remembered because the Scots won. Unlike Flodden and Culloden, an army of Scots, fighting for a king of Scotland, put an army from over the border – an army consisting of Englishmen, Welshmen and Europeans as well as Scots – to ignominious flight. The songs of Scotland would in later years consist primarily of threatening rants and poignant dirges. In Bannockburn the Scots have something to celebrate: a victory.

The fact that Bannockburn was for the Scots a victory to be celebrated and for the English a defeat to be excused has been the major encumbrance for those who have since described the battle. First, its importance has been exaggerated by both sides. The Scots have made Bannockburn into the Yorktown of Scotland, that battle which finally decided the question of Scottish sovereignty. The English have made Bannockburn into a colossal failure of generalship and organisation, which resulted in a vast improvement in English military practice, which, in turn, resulted in the victories at Crécy, Agincourt and Waterloo.

There is one other reason why the Battle of Bannockburn has captured the general imagination. The story of the battle is a rattling good yarn. The story of Bannockburn is filled with tales of bravery, stupidity and bloody murder. There is sex, violence and terror. The shepherd lad has a chance to hoist his banner and rout the foe, and the knight has a chance to save his king, then charge to glorious death. There is a long, tense night spent scanning the woods for the enemy known to be lurking there. There is an almost cinematic scene of an army coming at dawn, like Birnham Wood, from nowhere. That is why I have set down this battle. I have told what factors coloured previous accounts and now I tell you what colours my account: the drama, the excitement, the almost literary quality of the Battle of Bannockburn.

Terminology

The language of modern military science, as taught in staff colleges the world over, is not suited to describing medieval battles accurately. Just as modern diagrams of battles depict groups of men as boxes moving from place to place along arrows, modern military terminology reduces the experience of a battle to a series of ciphers. Since so many military historians have, in the past, been military men who have been schooled to describe battles with the terminology of the staff college, a great deal of military writing has been filled with the corresponding preconceptions. I have therefore tried to eschew inappropriate use of modern military terminology.

There are some terms which modern military science has developed which are useful in describing a medieval battle, as well as ancient terms which also have modern meanings. When I use these terms I risk attaching modern preconceptions to medieval facts. For the convenience of calling a low-level supervisor of soldiers a 'sergeant', however, it is worth risking confusion with the 'servientes', the lesser horsemen who gave the sergeant his name.

I have generally used the term 'front' to refer to the direction facing the enemy. 'Advancing' is moving towards the enemy, and 'retreating' is moving away from the enemy. These terms must be viewed without modern judgements attached, and without considering their precise technical meanings. For example, in discussing a Napoleonic army, 'front' is an almost sacred direction of reference, and an army in column of march generally faces right, and marches with 'front' on its left.

Nomenclature

Anglo-Norman and Norman-Scottish noblemen had Christian names (like Edward, Pain or Marmaduke) given at christening; surnames (like Barclay, de Tiptoft or Thweng) which were generally patronymic, as well as titles (like Sir or the Earl of Gloucester) which were inherited or conferred. Even one man's name and title can vary from one text to the next, or even within a text. I have attempted to standardise names as much as possible, using the modern first name, surname format and English names (e.g. Ingraham de Umfraville and Thomas Gray). In the case of earls and bishops I have used their titles, save where I wished to emphasise their family connections. One such special case is Gilbert Clare, Earl of Gloucester and Hertford, who was related to everybody, and who will be called both Clare and Gloucester. Where possible I have used nicknames, since they tend to be much more distinctive than Christian names. It is unfortunate, however, that none of Edward II's nicknames has been fit to record, so we must just call him Edward of Caernarvon.

Money

The basic unit of money in England was the silver penny (d for the Latin *denarius*), which weighed 22 grains, or about 1.4g. It could be cut into four quarters called farthings. Twelve pence made a shilling (s for the Latin *sestertius*). Thirteen shillings and fourpence made a mark (⅔ of a pound). Twenty shillings (two hundred and forty pence) made a pound (£ for the Latin *libra*). A pound represented one Troy pound's weight of silver (about 373g). There were no pound or shilling coins until the seventeenth and sixteenth centuries, respectively. A mark also represented a specific weight of silver: eight ounces Troy (about 249g). Silver exchanged at various rates with gold, such as the English gold penny, which weighed 45 grains (about 2.9g) and was worth one shilling and eightpence (twenty silver pence) in 1257, and two shillings (twenty-four silver pence) in 1265. There was no copper coin.

Note on Sources

I have not used academic referencing in this work. In reading a work of popular history, I find it awkward always to be referring to reference notes, and I see no purpose to using them here. Should the reader seek an academic work on the subject, I refer him to the bibliography at the end of this work. In particular I recommend G.W.S. Barrow's work on Robert Bruce for its rigorous treatment of the Bannockburn material.

I

The Significance of Bannockburn

Kingship of Scotland

The first king of Scotland worthy of the title was Kenneth, son of Alpin, who in the year 843 murdered the earls of Dalriada and absorbed the lands of the Picts, lately massacred by Norse raiders. Kenneth was descended from a family which emigrated from Ireland. From the year 921, the Anglo-Saxon kings in England claimed Scotland as part of their imagined pan-British dominion. Kings of Scotland from 921 onwards gave their allegiance to English kings when it suited them, and ignored their theoretical overlords most of the time.

The colourful line of Scottish kings ran in a more or less steady and bloody line from Alpin. The line suffered a seventeen-year kink when Macbeth sat on the throne, but that interregnum ended with the coronation of Malcolm Ceanmore in 1057. The crown danced between brothers and sons, marrying into the Norwegian and English royal lines, and landed in the dust in the year 1286 when Alexander III fell from his horse and died.

Alexander III's granddaughter, Margaret the Maid of Norway, was theoretically queen regnant from 1286 to 1290.

Margaret ascended the throne at the age of three, and was betrothed to young Edward Plantagenet of Caernarvon (the future King Edward II of England). On her way from Norway (her father was King Erik of Norway) to her coronation and wedding she died at sea, leaving Scotland in the hands of a regency council made up of warring Scottish noblemen.

The language of the betrothal between Margaret and Prince Edward implied a Plantagenet lordship over Scotland. King Edward I, Edward Longshanks, had just completed the conquest of Wales and was eager for more worlds to win. Scotland was vulnerable, in the hands of feuding lords. Thus began the wars that are called the Scottish Wars of Independence.

The Siege of Stirling

Scotland is divided by culture and by the Grampian Mountains into two distinct parts: the Highlands in the north and west and the Lowlands in the south and east. This division has survived to this day, although the linguistic and cultural differences that made the division a stark one have faded somewhat in the course of years. This is not the only division of Scotland, however. Running down from the southern range of the Grampians is the River Forth, which flows eastward into the Firth of Forth, an inlet of the North Sea. This river and the firth divide the Lowlands into northern and southern parts.

Even before the modern Firth of Forth Bridge was built, this division could be crossed. It was possible for a small party to make a laborious trek upriver, and splash across the Forth where it is narrow, above the tidal reaches. It was possible to row a boat across the Firth of Forth or across the River Forth, and a regular ferry service is indicated by nearby place-names like Queensferry. Taking an army across was a different matter: possible, but difficult. An astonishing number of boats and barges would have been necessary in order to do this with any speed, and the boats and men needed to be carefully marshalled in order to do this at all. Edward I once towed three pontoon bridges by sea, in order to cross quickly. Taking an army upriver through the hills, where there were no roads to speak of, was difficult as well. Another military option was a slow, dangerous fording just upriver of Stirling Bridge, where an army was sure to be seen and opposed, slaughtered as they tried to clamber up the muddy banks at low tide.

The River Forth flows down from the mountains near Ben Lomond, and runs out into the rolling hills of the Lowlands near Stirling. The elevation of the riverbank there is so low that the tides flood the river and tidal bogs twice a day, though the North Sea is many miles away. Just below the mountains, at the tidal line, where the river is narrow and does not flood twice a day, there is a point where a medieval engineer could build a bridge. The point is overlooked by a great table of rock, and on this rock is built the fortress of Stirling. To take an army into the northern Lowlands it was necessary to march to Stirling, under the shadow of Stirling Castle, and across that one bridge. Stirling thus controlled military access to the northern area of the Scottish Lowlands. Every southern general to campaign in Scotland has had to cross Stirling Bridge. Only seventeen years before Bannockburn, in September 1297, William Wallace defeated a Plantagenet army as it attempted to cross there. The fortress at Stirling was continually garrisoned. This is comparable to London, where London Bridge was for centuries the only place an army could cross from the south of England to the east. There the Tower of London controlled access between Surrey and Kent on the south bank, and Essex on the north bank.

King Edward II needed to control the Lowlands in order to protect the north of England from Scottish raids, and in order to maintain the Plantagenet claim of overlordship over Scotland. In order to control the Lowlands he needed to communicate with and re-supply his fortresses there. Stirling was the keystone of this chain of fortresses, since no army could cross the bridge there without the leave of the governor of Stirling. Robert Bruce's campaign of 1313 attempted to destroy this chain of fortresses, one by one. It was important to destroy these castles: Robert could not afford troops and loyal commanders to garrison them, and if they fell back into English hands all his work would be undone.

When his brother, Edward Bruce, Earl of Carrick, laid siege to Stirling, his job was to destroy the garrison, either by starvation or by tempting them to battle, then to destroy the fortress. Carrick's opponent in this was Sir Philip Mowbray, a Scottish knight who was the English king's governor of Stirling. Mowbray saw that no relief was imminent. Furthermore it was June, and several months of good campaigning weather remained before Carrick would need to send his men home for the harvest and the winter. Mowbray faced a gruelling summer of war and hunger, and he saw a way to avoid it.

Mowbray rode out of the gates of Stirling to propose a bargain. As it was, Carrick's army would be tied up in a long and uncomfortable siege. He would be forced to denude the surrounding countryside all summer in order to feed his men, and then send them home in the autumn, possibly without starving the garrison out of Stirling. The bargain: if Carrick called his army off and allowed Mowbray to re-supply the castle, Mowbray would keep his men inside and not interfere with traffic on Stirling Bridge. If no English army came within three leagues (14.5km, 9 miles, or about half a day's march) of Stirling in a year and a day, Mowbray would surrender the fortress, just as though the army had been laying costly siege for an entire year.

The Earl of Carrick had before him an offer of bloodless victory. For the entire campaign season the bridge would be open, and instead of spending the good months of 1313 twiddling his thumbs in camp, he could reduce a different fort. Next year the situation could be different, with the successes of 1313 bringing new allies. Even if the unpopular Edward II could raise an army and march it to Scotland, he would find a hard-running fight with great potential for defeat and ransom.

Carrick agreed. In a chivalric bargain the two knights accepted Mowbray's plan, and the Plantagenet's man was given safe conduct to go to London and warn King Edward. Edward Bruce sent messengers to his brother to bring the good news.

King Robert Bruce was not impressed. Although his brother had arranged for the bloodless surrender of an important castle, the surrender was by no means certain. Before, the fate of the English garrisons was in the hands of a few starving soldiers at Stirling, now the English had time to raise an army of relief. If the Earl of Carrick had taken

Stirling, the English army might still have come, but it would have chased the Scottish armies around the countryside, while Stirling remained a pile of rubble. Now the fortress would be intact, and in order to take it from Mowbray, King Robert would be forced to meet the relieving army.

King Robert could not count on his previous guerrilla tactics. Those had been effective on the small feudal forces raised by King Edward's allies in Scotland. On a campaign that would certainly be a thrust to Stirling followed by a re-establishing of the old English fortresses, likely to be conducted by a large army of the sort that had just recently won all of Wales for the Plantagenets, small-scale tactics of hit and run might weaken the army, but would not have time to bleed it dry.

The Earl of Carrick had forced his brother to make a stark choice. Either he must allow an English army to relieve Stirling, and resign free travel between the north and south Lowlands, or he must abandon his guerrilla tactics to meet an English army in an open battle.

2

Edward II Plantagenet, King of England

But there's a saying, very old and true,
'If that you will France win,
Then with Scotland first begin':
For once the eagle England being in prey,
To her unguarded nest the weasel Scot
Comes sneaking, and so sucks her princely eggs;
Playing the mouse in absence of the cat,
To spoil and havoc more than she can eat.

King Henry V, William Shakespeare

The Plantagenets were reputed to have been descended on one side from Satan via Melusine, his daughter. More directly, they were descended from Geoffrey Plantagenet, the count of Anjou and Maine. Geoffrey's nickname 'Plantagenet' is variously ascribed to his being compared to a genet, which is a sort of civet cat, or to his habit of wearing a broom on his head (genet is a sort of broom plant). Geoffrey married Matilda, who was on the rebound from her first husband, the Holy Roman Emperor. Their heir was called Henry fitz Empress, the second Henry since the Conquest. Best known for having had too many sons, Henry ruled one of the largest empires seen in western Europe in the Middle Ages, and developed a mechanism for the English state which survived the neglect of his son Richard Lionheart and only fell apart under the gifted meddling of his son John Lackland. John Lackland's son was Henry III, who was a Good King, and known primarily for surviving the revolt of Simon Montfort and for receiving an elephant as a gift. His son and heir was Edward Longshanks, who in spite of all the Anglo-Saxon King Edwards who came before him is called Edward the First.

King Edward Longshanks, the Hammer of the Scots, is considered a 'Good King'. He did not lose any land in France, he did not get mired in Ireland and he turned Wales from a troublesome land on his western flank into a wholly owned and operated subsidiary of the English crown. He spent a great deal of time in England without any serious damage to the monarchy's power or its treasury. He married twice, and produced enough sons that even when the eldest few died, he still had an heir to follow him. Longshanks expelled England's Jews, and while this puts him in danger of being called a Bad King by some, the Jews were probably better off elsewhere.

Edward Longshanks ruled with a gusto that did not always impress his noblemen. He was always willing to take an army over to France or Flanders, Wales or Scotland, whether his English peers liked it or not. He taxed his kingdom heavily to pay for these operations, including his clergy. In addition to relying on diplomacy and the feudal obligations of the nobles, he financed his operations by hiring mercenaries on credit.

For most of his reign his nobles were ready to follow their king to war, and help foot the bill. However, the heavy taxation, combined with royal attempts to homogenise the administration of the kingdom at the expense of noble privileges, caused some disenchantment. To quiet the kingdom, Longshanks apologised publicly for the taxation, then went ahead with expensive wars. When his nobles forced him to confirm the Magna Carta and the Forest Charter, which demanded the consent of the lords, the bishops and the commons for any taxes, he consented just as long as they were powerful enough to insist. Once back in the catbird seat he reasserted his authority, and discarded his agreements. When it was convenient he arranged for papal absolution from his confirmation. He was the king, after all.

Longshanks was king of England during the flowering of chivalric romance. As ruler of a good deal of France, he was exposed to the troubadour tradition that had provided the mythic basis for high medieval chivalry. Prominent amongst these traditions was the Matter of Britain (along with the Matter of France, which concerned Charlemagne and the Matter of Rome, which concerned Rome). The Matter of Britain was a cycle of the legends of King Arthur and the knights of the Round Table. To the medieval mind, there was no doubt of King Arthur's existence, just as there was no doubt about Jonah's having been swallowed by a fish. King Arthur was the greatest ruler England ever knew, ruling an empire which stretched from Ireland across western Europe to Rome (where, according to Geoffrey of Monmouth, he was elected emperor by the Senate). This cycle of legend was popular in France (where people preferred to think of Arthur as a Breton rather than a Briton), and it was especially popular with King Edward I, who seems to have seen Arthur as his model.

Longshanks convened round tables, he held feasts with chained swans, he surrounded himself with young knights and he set about unifying Great Britain under his control, no doubt preparatory to bagging France and beginning to work his way south to Rome and a purple toga. His Welsh campaigns were effective, eliminating the last native sovereigns of Wales. He built huge fortresses to control the Welsh, including one at Caernarvon where his fourth son was born. He turned his attention to Scotland with similar single-minded concentration. His campaigns were models of military excellence, and they displayed a pragmatic willingness to ignore the conventions of chivalric combat in return for success. While the tactical successes of the Welsh Wars might be credited to various generals, the policy of putting victory before tradition must have owed a great deal to the king.

Edward of Caernarvon

Longshanks's fourth son, Edward of Caernarvon, was born in Wales in 1284, the year of his final conquest of that troublesome country. Longshanks's eldest son, Alfonso (Longshanks had married a Castilian princess), died in that same eventful year, after his two next younger brothers. Edward was left as heir to the throne of the Plantagenet empire, which included not only England but also Wales and the French territories of Gascony, Ponthieu and Aquitaine. He seems to have been left alone with his nurse and his noble young friends until he turned fifteen, though his hand in marriage was traded back and forth, and he was theoretically regent of England when his father was away doing the trading. In 1299 (aged fifteen) he was betrothed to the eight-year-old Princess Isabella of France, while old Longshanks (sixty years old, to be precise) married Isabella's seventeen-year-old aunt. At sixteen

Edward was brought along on his father's unremarkable campaign in Scotland which ended after the successful siege of Carlaverock. At seventeen he was made Prince of Wales and Earl of Chester, giving him his own bench in Parliament, though the revenues from his Welsh lands seem to have continued to go to his father's treasury at Westminster.

It seems that Edward Longshanks was not impressed with his offspring, but was determined to make the best of what he had. He began to train his boy to be a proper Plantagenet knight and king. After a falling-out with his father, the younger Edward was reconciled with the elder in 1305, and in 1306 he was knighted in preparation for the new Scottish war. As well, he was made Duke of Aquitaine and Count of Ponthieu. All this was in time for Prince Edward and an army of young English knights to march northwards separately from the main English army, behaving badly as they went. It was on this campaign that Robert Bruce was turned by means of his enemies' unchivalrous tricks from Anglo-Norman earl into a king of Scots with no kingdom (more about that later).

Another falling-out occurred that winter of 1306, when Prince Edward bullied a bishop into asking that the county of Ponthieu be given to his boyhood friend Piers Gaveston. Longshanks raged at his son, and made it clear that he was tolerated for the good of the Plantagenet empire, and not for his own virtues.

Prince Edward of Caernarvon would later become King Edward II, known to the popular imagination as a Bad King. In addition to being a Bad King, Edward II seems to have had all the personality faults that the Plantagenets' contemporaries saw as signs of descent from the Old Man himself. Young Edward's ideas of filial piety were displayed at Burgh-on-Sands. There, as old Longshanks lay dying he asked that his heart be taken from his body and brought to the Holy Land on crusade to fulfil an oath he had sworn years before. Some say he also asked that his bones be taken on campaign in Scotland. Young King Edward II saw fit to do none of these, sending the body of the Hammer of the Scots to Waltham instead of Jerusalem. The new king followed southwards soon after, the campaign in Scotland forgotten.

The Most Annoying Man in England

The most celebrated analysis applied to Edward of Caernarvon is that he was a homosexual and allowed his relationships to impinge upon his conduct both as heir and as king. The evidence for this is his close friendship with Piers Gaveston, and his later friendship with Hugh Despenser and his father, Hugh senior. This is supported by the theory, widely believed then as now, that King Edward II was killed by being buggered with a hot poker (which is seen as a sort of prosaically crude poetic justice). This is further supported by contemporary chroniclers' accusations of sodomy, veiled and otherwise. As to his relationships with Gaveston and the elder and younger Despensers, these were certainly damaging to Edward's power and prestige. It must be remembered, however, that unlike our enlightened days when practised homosexuality is no bar to public office, the medieval Church and community frowned on buggery and sodomy. One of the accusations levied against the Knights Templars at about this time was that they practised organised homosexuality. It may have been that stories of his homosexual practices were spread by those who disapproved of King Edward for other

reasons, regardless of the Plantagenet's actual sexual prefer-
ence. It seems especially odd that close friendships with men
should be so strongly condemned, when the (chaste) friendship of a knight and his mates was so idealised by theorists of
chivalry. Perhaps the idea of knights preferring the company
of other knights in brotherhood was just so much chin music,
no more a fact of life in the fourteenth century than was the
'courtly love' that told young men to chastely love women
and have no thoughts of sex.

There is no doubt that Edward of Caernarvon had his
favourites, and the most notable of these was Gaveston, a
Gascon, and thus a subject of the Plantagenet empire. He is a
prime candidate for the honour of being the most disliked
man in English history; he has the advantage of being eligible
for non-partisan hatred (unlike Oliver Cromwell), of being
justly hated (unlike Richard III) and of having actually lived
(unlike the Sheriff of Nottingham). He is distinguished by
having been so obnoxious that he was banished perpetually
from England by Longshanks, in order to keep him from
becoming a menace to public order. He seems to have been
killed purely because he was so annoying. The most unpopular act of Edward II's reign was to invite him back to England
before Longshanks's body was even cold.

Precisely why Piers Gaveston was so annoying is unclear.
No single personality trait of his seems obnoxious enough to
justify the hatred he earned. It appears that he was just so personally abrasive that it was a labour to suffer his presence. He
made up insulting nicknames for the powerful barons, and
used them to taunt these nobles from the protection of his
royal patron's shadow. Since this is just the only recordable
manifestation of his lack of social skills, one's imagination

must construct a man so annoying that a committee of earls put their property and their very lives at risk in forming a cabal to connive his death.

It did not help Edward that one of his first acts on the death of his father was to recall Gaveston to England. Longshanks had attempted to guard against this eventuality by making the Earl of Lancaster and other nobles swear that the Gascon should never be allowed to return. Instead, with Longshanks safely in his vault, Gaveston was married off to a Clare daughter and made Earl of Cornwall, which again infuriated the earls who were jealous of their status as the premier noblemen of the kingdom (there were no English duchies then). When Edward went to France on Longshanks's death to marry his betrothed, he left Gaveston in charge as regent in his absence, further inflaming the earls.

For a while Gaveston was sent to Ireland at the earls' insistence. The Archbishop of Canterbury contributed a conditional excommunication, effective only if Gaveston returned to England. A period of frenzied diplomacy resulted, in which Edward literally moved heaven and earth to bring Gaveston back. He convinced the Pope to use his key to the kingdom of heaven and overrule the conditional excommunication. The king bribed some of the earls with favours and lands to accept the Gascon's return. King Edward recalled Gaveston, who was full of himself after putting down some Irish rebellions, and who was no less obnoxious than he had been before. In 1312 he returned unasked from a brief banishment by the Lords Ordainers (of whom more later), and King Edward restored the earldom of Cornwall to his pet. Edward even tried to bargain with Robert Bruce to ensure Gaveston's safety.

By now everyone's patience had been exhausted. Canterbury excommunicated the Gascon. Every earl in England was ready to overthrow the king in defence of the Ordinances and in spite of Gaveston. Only Gloucester, childhood friend of both King Edward and Piers Gaveston, nephew of the king and brother-in-law of the hated Gascon (and friend and cousin of King Robert of Scots, by the way), held out, until he too was persuaded to join the earls in planning an uprising.

The earls pursued the king and his favourite. In his haste to get his friend to safety, Edward even abandoned his pregnant wife Isabella at Tynemouth, where she was captured by the Earl of Lancaster. At last the king and Gaveston separated, and the latter went to ground in Scarborough Castle. The Earl of Pembroke took the castle by bargain, and began to conduct the unhappy Gascon to his trial at the next parliament. While Pembroke was conveniently looking away, Gaveston was arrested by the Earl of Warwick who turned him over to the Earl of Lancaster who had him killed by thugs. Because he was the Earl of Cornwall the thugs took care to cut his head off, in mockery of the execution reserved for noblemen.

Instead of cutting his losses and backing off from his enraged earls, King Edward attempted to destroy Lancaster by fomenting a revolt in his home county of Lancashire. This trick failed miserably, but succeeded in distracting King Edward while King Robert and his friends levied blackmail throughout the north and enforced their rackets with burning and plundering.

It did not endear King Edward to his nobles that he was not fond of warfare. While modern monarchs are encouraged to have hobbies, to take their minds off the fact that they have a great deal of spare time, this was not so for medieval kings.

Sailor-kings, for instance, are only recently fashionable; and the English nobles were disgusted that Edward enjoyed spending his time learning basic navigation and messing about in boats. He also indulged in other common pursuits like building, thatching and digging, whereas knights were expected to spend their time conducting wars and breaking heads.

One is struck by the thought that Edward of Caernarvon's life would have been a long and happy one had one of his elder brothers survived to assume the burden of the crown, and left him to live as an extra prince, married to an inconsequential English noblewoman, with nothing to do but go swimming and fishing with his friends.

The She-Wolf of France

Edward of Caernarvon was married to a woman called Isabella, the She-Wolf of France. This nickname does not seem auspicious, and the appearance is not deceptive. When she was repeatedly rejected by her husband in favour of male favourites, she struck at her royal husband like an angry beast, and attacked him politically, militarily and even sexually. It is not difficult to understand her feelings. Married to the young Plantagenet king by diplomatic arrangement, she thought she could at least look forward to being the centre of attention at her Westminster coronation a month later. She would wear the royal jewels and spend her honeymoon with a good-looking prince. In the event, Piers Gaveston wore the queen's jewels – indeed he was dressed more stunningly – and while Edward did indeed do his marital duty by Isabel, producing the son who would succeed him while he still lived, he preferred to pay attention to his male darlings.

Except for a brief period of reconciliation after the death of Gaveston and before Hugh Despenser was elevated to the status of Chief Royal Pet, there was a constant antagonism between Edward and the She-Wolf. As it became clear that Edward preferred the company of Despenser to that of his wife, Isabel cheated on him with Roger Mortimer, and eventually plotted his overthrow with Mortimer's connivance.

Saint Thomas of Lancaster

Edward's marital problems came to a head only late in his career. Problems with his earls began much earlier. The Earl of Lancaster was the most powerful earl in England. With his base of three counties, increased in 1311 by two when the Earl of Lincoln died, he could afford to plague Edward continually with rebellions. Lancaster had no difficulty finding allies against the king.

The earls began to impose reforms on the king. In 1309 they restricted the Crown's power to set prices for military victuals. They took many of the offices of central government out of the royal household. In 1310 the earls imposed on Edward a council of overseers called the Lords Ordainers. This committee was an interesting mix of two earls who were chosen by bishops, two bishops chosen by earls, two barons picked by the four chosen earls and bishops, and fifteen others elected by the first six, for a total of twenty-one. The Lords Ordainers imposed forty-one Ordinances on the king, decrying the king's evil counsellors and especially Piers Gaveston. As well, the Ordinances condemned and ordered exile for the king's Italian banker, Frescobaldi, in an attempt to control the king's ability to raise funds without the consent of a parliament. The administration of the kingdom was also regulated by the Ordinances, requiring parliamentary approval of the officers of the kingdom (such as the Chancellor of the Exchequer) and of the king's household. Unpopular taxes like Longshanks's duties on wool were also repealed, and the king was placed on an austere budget controlled by the Exchequer.

The Ordinances are a well-thought-out series of reforms, though modern economic historians doubt the wisdom of some provisions. They are quite evidently not merely a grab for more individual power for the earls, nor are they merely an arrow shot at Piers Gaveston. Longshanks had discarded his Confirmation of the Charters, which affirmed barons' rights. Edward II had reversed two banishments of Gaveston. These reforms, finally promulgated in 1311, were not so easy to wriggle out of.

When King Edward allowed Gaveston to return to England in spite of the Ordinances, all the earls rose up and enforced the decision of the Ordainers by capturing and executing Gaveston. The rift was patched up when Lancaster gave the king Gaveston's copious goods, and in return for a full pardon the earls apologised for killing the Gascon. Lest anyone think the wound was fully healed, the king and the Earl of Lancaster feasted separately to celebrate the reconciliation.

The End

After Bannockburn it only got worse for Edward II. When he called a parliament, his nobles came with large, menacing liveried retinues. Notable amongst these nobles were Mowbray, who had been governor of Stirling before Bannockburn, and Clifford, who had commanded a battalion at the battle. A concord with Lancaster was short-lived. King Edward's belated attempts to attack the Scots in the north were met with the usual Scottish tactics of evasion. Since the Scots had extended their power through Cumberland and Northumberland, it lost them little to scorch the English earth as they retreated . It seems that Edward was unable to resurrect the complex system of provisioning that he had planned for his Stirling campaign of 1314, and the king had to cut off the campaign for lack of provisions. He returned from the north to more rebellion from his barons and his queen, and fought a war of mercurial fortunes: first besieged by the She-Wolf and the barons; then capturing and executing his enemies, including the Earl of Lancaster. This gave him leisure to conduct a disastrous campaign against the Scots (in 1322) which ended with the Scots sacking all the way to York.

The steep decline of Edward II's reign after 1322 (the high point of his reign had been the execution of Lancaster in that year) is too complicated and miserable to discuss at length here. He began by acquiring Hugh Despenser as a replacement favourite for Gaveston. Lancaster became, in the popular imagination, St Thomas of Lancaster, martyred in the cause of enforcing good government. His grave at Pontefract was a place of pilgrimage, and his brother the Earl of Leicester, once reconciled to the Plantagenet, became increasingly unreliable. Now the She-Wolf was in Paris, with her brother, the king of France. She was also living with Roger Mortimer, in spite of her marriage. The tension grew greater, with English nobles siding with either the king and Despenser or the queen and her bishops. Edward's son, the young Duke of Aquitaine, was knocked back and forth between the English parties and the king of France.

When the king sent a message to the She-Wolf, asking her to return to England, she did, bringing with her an army, which picked up followers as it marched west to London. King Edward proceeded to lose battles at a furious rate, retreating across the breadth of England and Wales. Weather conditions made it impossible for him to flee across the Irish Sea, and he found himself captured and interned. Since he would not abdicate in parliament, the clever lawyers' trick of Articles of Deposition was devised. Under the threat that the articles would be applied to his son as well, setting Mortimer not only in his bed but on his throne, King Edward II abdicated. Deposed by his wife, aided by her lover, in favour of his son Edward, Duke of Aquitaine (Edward III), Edward Plantagenet, private citizen, became a symbol of the Good Old Days. After his death in September 1327, his tomb in Gloucester Cathedral was revered as a shrine, and Edward II joined his arch-enemy Thomas of Lancaster as an informal English saint.

Edward met a bad end, which history has regarded with smug satisfaction. After his overthrow by wife and son, he was dragged from castle to castle, ending up in Berkeley. There he was starved, but he did not die quickly enough. Legend has it that Edward of Caernarvon was hastened to his reward by having a red-hot soldering iron inserted into his abdomen via a tube in his anus. Thus his murderers intended that no outward mark would remain as evidence of foul play. It is ironic that although Bannockburn can be considered the greatest defeat of English arms in the Middle Ages, it was the least of King Edward's personal defeats.

3

Robert the Bruce, King of Scotland

Robert Bruce, the Earl of Carrick, arranged a meeting with the Red Comyn, John Lord of Badenoch, at Greyfriars Church in Dumfries on 10 February 1306.

These two competitors for the throne of Scotland had made a deal: in return for some land, the Comyn would cede the throne to the Bruce. The Comyn had betrayed this bargain to the king of England, telling King Edward that evidence of the bargain would follow. Gilbert de Clare, the young Earl of Gloucester and Hertford, learned of the Red Comyn's message, and sent a message of his own to his friend and cousin Robert Bruce who was also attending the English court. Gloucester's message consisted of a gift of 12 pence and a pair of spurs, a clear enough hint. Bruce was gone before morning.

Along his way, Bruce encountered the Comyn's messenger to the English king, bringing by way of evidence the contract between the Bruce and the Red Comyn that established their bargain. It was to discuss this betrayal that Robert had arranged to meet with the Comyn at the altar of Greyfriars Church. The two great men withdrew to speak on the neutral ground of the altar, and there the argument was settled.

Bruce wounded the Red Comyn with a knife, and as his uncle Robert Comyn tried to intervene he was cut down by Bruce's brother-in-law, Christopher Seton. As the Bruce left the church, Roger Kirkpatrick and James Lindsay went in to make sure of the death of Robert Bruce's only rival for the Scottish throne.

Robert the Myth

There is a hill in modern Jerusalem that was bought from the Greek Orthodox Patriarchate at the beginning of the twentieth century. There, facing across the Hinnom Valley towards Dormition Abbey on Mount Zion, is an imposing church. Flying from the building's tower is the blue and white flag of Scotland. Inside the church, within the plain sanctuary and just before a communion table inlaid with rock from the sacred isle of Iona, is a great plaque commemorating the heart of a Scottish king.

Evelyn, the kindly Scottish missionary who acts as secretary of the church, explains to visitors that Robert the Bruce, the vanquisher of the English, was dying of leprosy when he asked his friend the Black Douglas to fulfil his lifelong vow to go on crusade by taking his heart to the Holy Land. Evelyn explains that the Bruce's body is in Dunfermline, and his heart rests in Melrose. All the same, here in Jerusalem, in a church opened by General Allenby, the hero of the Last Crusade, a plaque marks the intent of a king to fulfil a vow, and a friend's intention to fulfil a dying wish.

What makes King Robert such a strong mythic figure? Part of the answer is that King Robert was able to set himself up as king of Scotland in the face of strong opposition and in spite of crushing reversals. Part is that Robert Bruce has been characterised in the popular imagination as a Scottish patriot, perhaps the first prominent Scottish patriot to fight the English on a large scale and live to die in his bed.

The Family Bruce

Saint Malachy, Archbishop of Armagh in Ireland, went on a pilgrimage to Rome in the year 1148. On his way, he passed through Annandale, and was hosted by the second Robert Bruce in the town of Annan. Malachy begged Christian mercy from Sir Robert for a man accused of thievery, and the lord of Annandale consented. The next day, as the holy man rode forth to continue on his journey, he saw the thief's body twisting on the end of a rope. In righteous rage, Saint Malachy revoked his blessing on the house, and pronounced his curse on Robert Bruce's line.

On 11 July 1274, at Turnberry in Clydesdale, Robert Bruce VII was born to Robert Bruce VI (lord of Annandale) and Marjorie of Carrick. The resulting patrimony included the adjacent lands of Annandale and Carrick in the west of Scotland, and made the infant Robert a wealthy lad indeed. Descended from Norse earls of Orkney who had departed for greener pastures in Normandy and then in England, the Bruces were an integral part of the Anglo-Norman aristocracy that ruled England and much of Scotland. Robert's great-grandfather, Robert Bruce IV, had married the daughter of the Earl of Huntingdon (a younger son of the king of Scotland). Robert's grandfather, Robert Bruce V the Competitor, had married Isabel de Clare, daughter of the Earl of Gloucester, and had tied his interests closely to those of the English king.

When the future King Robert was eighteen his father (Robert Bruce VI) resigned the earldom of Carrick, and Robert became Earl in his place. Old Robert faded into obscurity, occasionally showing up at an English parliament, and possibly going on crusade. It is significant that Robert Bruce did not take any overt action against the king of England whilst his father lived. He bided his time until his father was dead and he was safe from dishonour and punishment.

> But that the Scot in his unfurnish'd kingdom
> Came pouring like the tide into a breach,
> With ample and brim fullness of his force;
> Galling the gleanèd land with hot assays,
> Girding with grievous siege castles and towns;
> That England, being empty of defense,
> Hath shook and trembled at th' ill neighbourhood.

King Henry V, William Shakespeare

Scottish Dependence

The European Middle Ages were based on agriculture. In an agrarian context Scotland is a poor country indeed. Most of Scotland is inhospitable to crops, and even in the Middle Ages, before cities and industrial parks were built, much of what is modern arable land was covered in peat. The herdsmen, fishermen and husbandmen who worked in Scotland had little left over after feeding and clothing their families, and the revenues of Scottish noblemen reflected this thin profit margin. The ways to wealth for a Scottish nobleman were either to take it from someone else or to garner estates in England. Most of them tried to do both. The object of the game for a Scots nobleman was to have as much power as possible in Scotland, in order to safeguard his Scottish possessions, without having so much that the English king felt threatened. If the English king needed to beat a Scottish nobleman into line, he need only threaten to take away his English estates, leaving him with only a few good farms and a great deal of rough pasturage.

This state of affairs created an interesting situation for the descendants of Alpin and Malcolm Ceanmore, the kings of Scots: exactly what were they king of? Much of the Highlands and the Isles were useless to a Norman-Scottish feudal landlord; the profit was in the herds or the fish and not the land. Thus it was hardly profitable for the king of Scots to go west to take on the vicious Irish tribes and their chiefs. The result was the rule of the chiefs in the Highlands and the Isles, and the man with the most ships controlled the Isles.

The Borders, those hilly tracts of poor land between Scotland and England, were also a law unto themselves. The Borders, like the Highlands, suffered from having portable wealth: cattle. It is unprofitable to destroy your enemy's farmland, and it is unprofitable for him to destroy yours. It is, however, quite profitable to rustle his cattle. The result is that the writ of the kings of Scots and England, based on the ownership of land, was equally worthless in the Borders, where once again tribal lords ruled.

In the Lowlands – the only part of Scotland that earned its keep for a feudal landlord – Norman-Scottish nobles were as beholden to the king of England as they were to the king of Scots. They journeyed to England when necessary to kneel in homage to the English king for their English estates, and this economic integration resulted in constant English political hegemony in Scotland.

It was natural, therefore, that the king of England should regard the king of Scotland as a subject prince. Indeed, the Parliament of Edward I had seats beside but below the English king for the king of Scotland and the Prince of Wales. Scottish kings had repeatedly made themselves vassals of English kings, and only the facts of history and British geography maintained a separate northern kingdom. Given the choice between expending his resources in increasing his control in Scotland or in fertile France, English kings always chose France. In essence, it was more trouble than it was worth to make Scotland a part of England.

The Church and Scotland

The Scottish Church was not interested in being tied to England. Scottish bishops and abbots were content to be big fish in their own little ecclesiastical pond, rather than to be incorporated into the vast sea of the English Church's Province of York. As the Scottish Church they constituted a small number of men, with a great deal of individual and collective power, responsible only to the distant Pope, as compared with the numerous members of the Convocation at York, which was sometimes in turn subject to the Archbishop of Canterbury in a complex web of sacerdotal primacy. Their revenues in Scotland did not need to be shared with their brethren in England, and their rulings on such political matters as fealty and marriage were not subject to English review. English episcopal appointments were dictated by the English king, and if ever he gained that power north of the Border, the Scottish bishops and abbots knew the appointments would go to English favourites and relatives, just as the king of England saw to the appointment of English priests to the smaller benefices in the Scottish lands he controlled. A weak but independent king of Scots, on the other hand, was not nearly so worrisome an intruder. So long as the king of Scots was, in fact or in law, a vassal of the king of England, the independence of the Scottish Church was in doubt, no matter how often Rome expounded upon Scottish independence.

One might wonder why the Pope of Rome was interested in the independence of the bishops of a resource-poor (and thus poor in tithes as well) kingdom like Scotland. This interest was due in part to the fact that the bishop of Rome had, since 1305, resided in Avignon. The fact of the Supreme Pontiff's residence in France had a great deal to do with French influence on Italian politics and very little to do with religion. At bottom, however, the Pope was both Vicar of Christ on Earth and a part-time employee of the king of France.

The complex politics of the early fourteenth century resulted in the Pope doing a dance on the sharp points of powerful interests: King Capet in France and Italy; King Plantagenet in France and England, who was no less powerful in France than the local king; King Bruce in Scotland, who was a pawn used by the king of France to threaten the king of England from the north; and the Scottish Church, which was used to prod the king of Scotland into his uncomfortable role.

An example of papal involvement in Anglo-Franco-Scottish relations, even before the 'Babylonian Captivity' in Avignon, was the reading in 1300 of Pope Boniface VIII's bull which repeated that Scotland was a fief not of England but of the Holy See. This was a result of Scottish diplomacy at the papal court in Rome, as well as the Pope's desire to be emperor of everything. This at a time when the English King Edward I was in an uneasy truce with his brother-in-law King Philip over the Plantagenet possessions in France, the English nobles were taking full advantage of the trouble to refuse military service, and the king of Scotland, John Balliol, was a prisoner of the Pope.

If this all seems too thick to be entirely comfortable, it certainly seemed that way to the king of France. After several years of extreme nastiness, France's desire to eliminate Boniface VIII's visions of papal grandeur resulted in the installation of the Gascon Clement V as Pope on an estate in Avignon (which was technically part of Naples, not France), and the incorporation of the papacy into the apparatus of the kingdom of France. Now, instead of throwing the weight of the papacy where it would do Rome the most good, the Pope threw his weight where it would do the king of France the most good. In general that included giving England a constant feeling of insecurity about its northern border, and in particular it meant allowing the Scottish bishops to keep the flame of Scottish sovereignty alive without allowing too much latitude in bending the rules of conduct that formed the cement of French as well as English society.

When Robert the Bruce had murdered his only serious rival to the throne in 1306, he went straightaway to Glasgow, where Bishop Wishart, whose primary occupation for the next decade would be living in English and papal gaols, gave the Bruce absolution for the sin of committing murder and sacrilege at Dumfries. In return for this public absolution, Robert swore an oath to preserve and defend the liberties of the Scottish Church. Bruce's coronation the next month at

Scone was attended by three bishops, all casting their ballots for an independent king of Scotland and an independent Church, responsible only to far-off Avignon.

The Crown of Scotland

One might wonder why the Scottish crown was available in that winter of 1306. One might easily conclude, after all, that the object of the great game that we call the feudal system was to be the king. Even when we recognise that medieval noblemen might virtuously decline to put themselves above their station in life, there must surely have been enough descendants of Fergus or Alpin to find someone willing to take the crown. Indeed, when King Robert's grandfather earned his nickname 'the Competitor' years before, there were no fewer than twelve claimants to the Scottish throne, clamouring for the crown vacated by Alexander III and his granddaughter, Margaret the Maid of Norway. It was at this time that the Bruce claim to the throne was first put on the family agenda, based on the same descent from David I that begot Alexander III's line. The reason for the vacancy has to do with a complicated set of circumstances that can be traced to the unfortunate road accident that killed King Alexander.

Scottish kings had traditionally been crowned upon the Stone of Destiny which legend had brought over from Tara, seat of Brian Boru, the High King of Ireland. This stone slab was kept at Scone, and Scottish kings were crowned sitting or standing thereon up until 1292 when John Balliol, vassal of King Edward I, was invested with the crown of Scotland. When King John was dispossessed by his overlord the king of England in 1296, he was taken to England, the Stone of Destiny with him, and it resided in Westminster until 1996. The king of England was no longer interested in having a dependent Scottish kingdom, since that sort of puppetry had proved ineffective. Instead, he preferred a military governor, John Warenne, the Earl of Surrey, whom he armed with a mass, sealed oath of fealty from everyone in Scotland who was anyone. This concluded the brutally effective Plantagenet campaign of 1296, assisted by one Robert Bruce VI, and his son Robert Bruce VII, Earl of Carrick, the great Scottish patriot and future king.

John Balliol's tabard, his heraldic surcoat with the red lion of Scotland within its distinctive fence of spear points, was torn from him by the bishop of Durham. Divested of the kingdom of Scotland, he lived out his life a prisoner and exile, nicknamed 'Toom Tabard' for the loss of his heraldic coat and the monarchy it represented. He died in 1313 while Robert Bruce, wearing John's old crown, was re-establishing the kingdom.

A Scottish nobleman who took up the crown of Alpin was a Scottish nobleman who resigned his fertile English lands and violated his oath of fealty to King Edward. As such, the banner of Scotland was taken up not by a nobleman, but by one William Wallace of Lanark, owner of some land at Paisley. The ubiquitous Wishart, bishop of Glasgow, who saw the prospect of the episcopal rule of York looming on the horizon, was in the process of inflaming Earl Robert Bruce, William Douglas and James Steward to small and unsuccessful feudal warfare against other English vassals. At the same time Wallace, who may or may not have been a professional brigand, started his career by killing the Plantagenet's Sheriff of Clydesdale. He went north to join an army being raised by Andrew de Moray, and attacked the English justiciar at Scone. Hugh Cressingham, who was financial deputy to the English governor, Surrey, responded by attacking Bruce, Douglas and Steward, and securing their surrender. Cressingham only went after the great nobles, without seeking Wallace. Wallace and his friends meanwhile declared themselves to represent old Toom Tabard, and with their army of brigands and outlaws ran rampant north of the Firth of Forth. When Cressingham went to Stirling in September 1297 to cross into the north of Scotland, the Wallace met him at Stirling Bridge. As the English knights rode three abreast from the bridge to the marshy ground beyond, the Wallace's humble army of pikes cut them up. Cressingham, known for his corpulence, was skinned, and his hide used for Wallace's scabbard, for riding tack and as tokens of the victory at Stirling Bridge.

Wallace had no English estates to lose, and he made a splendid guardian of Scotland, except that very few Scottish nobles were interested in following some common yob who had no more noble blood than their horse-grooms. He held a rough dominion over Scotland, with the English keeping to their castles and most of the Scottish nobles keeping to their estates, until Edward Longshanks came north in 1298. Longshanks had just made peace with the king of France, and he had an army available to send to Scotland. At Falkirk, only a day's march south and east of Stirling, the English met Wallace's spears, and the English archers and Gascon crossbowmen sent their equally common Scottish enemies fleeing. Wallace disappears from the sight of history for several years, and a ruling council of Robert the Bruce (the future King Robert I), the Red Comyn and the bishop of St Andrews was left in charge of Scotland on behalf of Longshanks, while the castles were manned by governors and garrisons loyal to the English king.

The ruling council dissolved into violent disagreement in short order, with the Bruce and the Comyn literally at each other's throats. Membership on the council shifted a bit, including then excluding Ingraham de Umfraville (the best of this whole lot of names). This instability invited a fresh invasion from the Plantagenet. Longshanks came in 1300, and aside from driving away some small attacks from the Comyn and other Scottish nobles, nothing was accomplished save the successful siege of Carlaverock, which was exalted in English song because there was nothing else to exalt. Because no large Scottish force attacked the Plantagenet's army, there was nobody for the English knights to fight with. Longshanks came again in 1301, and stayed until 1302, but he could find nobody to fight him.

On this occasion, Robert Bruce (still our Robert) submitted to and swore allegiance to King Edward. After all, Wallace was still claiming to guard Scotland on behalf of Toom Tabard, and that gave Bruce's head little hope for wearing the crown. Bruce was repaid for his submission in 1304, when Longshanks made him co-ruler of Scotland with the bishop of Glasgow and an English baron. Edward and this council worked out a system for the governance of Scotland as an English fief, under the Earl of Richmond as viceroy and a council of Scottish prelates and barons.

Stirling was once again the site of a battle in 1305, when an English siege, supported by the state of the art in siege engines, took the castle from one Sir William Oliphant, who held it for Wallace. There was a certain air of inevitability about the siege, with the English queen watching from Stirling Town with her ladies. Oliphant and his knights knelt in submission to the Plantagenet, and Scotland looked like a quiet English province.

When Wallace appeared again that same month, he was quickly betrayed to the English and dragged to London, tied to his horse. Wallace was charged with a list of crimes, including betraying his oath of fealty to Edward Plantagenet. He admitted all charges but the oathbreaking, pointing out quite reasonably that he had never taken an oath of fealty to Edward Plantagenet. William Wallace, the guardian of Scotland, was, to use the common euphemism, hanged, drawn and quartered, with burning and beheading thrown in for good measure.

The advisory committee appointed to await the coming of the new viceroy to Scotland was headed by the bishop of St Andrews. The bishop had been in France and in Rome lobbying for such favours as the bull which recognised Scotland as a papal fief. As we recall the Scottish Church's attitude towards English dominion, we might consider that the appointment of St Andrews to chair the English ruling committee might have been unwise on Edward I's part, but Longshanks did not have our benefit of hindsight.

Robert Bruce and his family were treated very well by King Edward. His brothers were given plum appointments, and he was allowed to consolidate his holdings at the expense of Ingraham de Umfraville (that splendid name again). When his father died in 1304, the thirty-year-old earl held large estates in Scotland and England, as well as a large Scottish wardship. As old King Edward grew older, making a fool of himself on military operations and becoming seriously ill, Robert saw the possibility of rejecting his patrimony in Huntingdonshire in favour of his patrimony in that slab of rock sitting under old Edward's chair in London. In 1304, with the show-siege of Stirling being played within sight, Robert Bruce and St Andrews concluded an alliance at

Cambuskenneth Abbey. The particular purpose of the alliance was not specified, but the primary interest that the subject earl and the subject bishop had in common was their subjection. Here, within a few minutes' walk of Stirling, the keystone of Scotland, the bishop of St Andrews threw his lot in with the Bruce. As Edward I's health failed further, Robert began the wheeling and dealing that would take him to that dim church at Dumfries, where the Red Comyn would bleed out his life on the altar stone.

A curious phenomenon of historical writing is the 'deathbed'. One is always forced to wonder how anyone knows in advance that any given bed is a 'deathbed'. Robert assumed that King Edward's failing health had removed him from the power equation: he assumed that Longshanks was on his deathbed. Robert, and the bishop of Glasgow, did not attend the English parliament in 1305 that was to ordain the governance of the land of Scotland. Whisperings in King Edward's suspicious old ear might have had something to do with the subsequent events: Robert must turn Kildrummy Castle over to a trusty man and Ingraham de Umfraville could have back his lands in Carrick. Bruce remained on the advisory council, however, where his influence was balanced by the presence of the Red Comyn.

The interregnum from the fall of Toom Tabard in 1296 to the murder of the Red Comyn in 1306 is considered by many the second phase of the 'War of Scottish Independence' (the interregnum between the death of Margaret the Maid of Norway and the coronation of Toom Tabard is considered the first). When one remembers that, in spite of a major English expenditure of money and effort, very little was accomplished in those ten years, it may be considered a war only from the point of view of English cost-accounting. As to independence, the Scotland of King Robert I and his successors was not much more nor much less unified or independent than the Scotland of the kings before Toom Tabard. The War of Independence lasted past Bannockburn, and indeed it might be extended (with a few long breaks) until 1746, when Scotland was forcibly unified at the cost of its independence.

Saint Malachy's Curse

Longshanks was a survivor. He had an ability to walk through accidents that Harold Lloyd would envy. When an assassin came for him in Palestine, he survived. When lightning struck his party in France, it shot past Edward and killed his friends. When he made a show of martial fervour at the Siege of Stirling, missiles struck his saddle and his horse, but missed him. Now he had a new challenge in Scotland, and he was not about to let his deathbed get in the way.

King Edward was still dying when he heard of the murder of the Red Comyn and the resulting disruption of the balance of power and destabilisation of Scotland. His fury at the Bruce's perfidy overcame his illness. He was carried on a horse-litter deathbed to London where he proceeded to knight his son Edward and as many other young squires as he could. His deathbed was then moved north to Carlisle, preceded by his army. The army sent him as prisoners the bishops of St Andrews and Glasgow – two of the three bishops of Scotland – leaving only the bishop of Moray to preach the Scottish monarchy.

The English army marched as far as the town of Perth while King Robert gathered an army of his own, mostly from the lowlands north of the Forth. At Methven, outside Perth, the Scottish king camped to await single combat the next day with the Earl of Pembroke, who commanded the English garrison. In the night the English and their Scottish allies broke Pembroke's chivalric word by attacking the Bruce camp, and the Bruce's small army was dispersed. The king himself escaped with a small number of his close friends, including James the Black, Earl of Douglas. The chivalric ethic was further dishonoured by the massacring of the captured knights without offer of ransom and without trial. Edward, Prince of Wales, and the other newly sworn knights mocked their knightly oaths, laying waste as they marched northwards.

Bruce now had a demonstration of the value of an English knight's chivalry. The ideals he had absorbed at the English court – ideals of courtesy, chivalry and decent treatment – were obviously not worth much to the English knight, and as Bruce settled down to years of hiding from his Scottish and English enemies he had a great deal to think about, especially concerning the gentlemanly proprieties of warfare. He took his family from Kildrummy westward towards Islay, where the Irish islemen might protect him. Along the way, as he received yet another absolution for his killing of the Red Comyn, he was attacked by the lord of Lorne, the dead Comyn's kinsman. Only by hard fighting did the Bruce and his family escape, with a wounded Black Douglas. Bruce gave up getting his wife and child to Islay, and instead sent them back to Kildrummy.

The women were captured, and caged or sent to nunneries. The men were executed. The Bruce knew none of this as he got to Dunaverty, to his ally Angus Og Macdonald. He fled further west, pursued by his enemies, landing on the tiny isle of Rathlin off the Irish coast, while far away at Lanercost Priory near Carlisle, on his mobile deathbed, King Edward I was passing sentence on his wife and his girl and the rest of his family and friends.

King Robert spent some two years haunting the west coast of Scotland in Angus Og's galleys, skulking ashore to collect his rents and striking out at his enemies when he could. Wherever he went he was betrayed, his only victories in small skirmishes. He heard the news of the caging of his little girl, of his sister and of his friend the Countess of Buchan, who had spited her Comyn husband to take the Earl of Fife's place at his coronation. He heard of his wife's imprisonment in a nunnery, saved from death only by the influence of her father, the Earl of Ulster. He heard of his brothers being hanged, drawn and quartered. He heard of the hanging of his friends Seton and Atholl. He thought of the dark presence of Edward Plantagenet, doing much better on his deathbed than Robert was doing in perfect health, and he compared this with his dominion of the entire isle of Rathlin. The gold of his crown seemed thin indeed.

King Robert huddled in the cave that was his royal castle, protected only by his anonymity, and considered his options. He could spend the rest of his life pretending to be king of Scotland, watching his friends killed one by one until the day the mad Englishman on that eternal deathbed at Lanercost had him hanged, drawn and quartered. On the other hand, he could chuck it all and go on crusade, expiating his sins with his death in a holy cause and ending the brooding presence of Saint Malachy's ancient curse. As he lay there he watched the perseverance of a spider weaving its web. Again and again the little creature tried to attach its silk to the walls, trying and failing until at last a web took shape. Whether Robert actually saw a real spider in that cave, or whether he or a later chronicler imagined it is unimportant. The important fact is that when he emerged from that cave, he emerged with resolve. King Robert vowed that if a horrid little spider could keep on trying, so could the grandson of Robert the Competitor, and he vowed that he would make himself king of Scotland.

The king of England's men pursued him with hounds, losing a skirmish here and winning one there. Here the Bruce gathered followers and there his followers were killed. He repeatedly distinguished himself as a fighting man during this period of lonely hiding. We have accounts of his taking on many men in combat, including a bloody tale of his holding a narrow ford single-handed, standing behind a rampart of dead horses and men, cutting his enemies down as they came in ones and twos. During this time only his own determination, the friendship of his remaining allies and the constant preaching of the Scottish priests, loyal to their captured prelates and to the bishop of Moray, kept alive the idea of a separate Scottish monarchy.

In May 1307, with Aylmer de Valence, the Earl of Pembroke, hot on his heels, King Robert's small body of foot soldiers turned to meet Pembroke near Loudon Hill. King Robert had dug trenches there to keep the English knights bunched closely together. The Scottish spearmen, formed in their shield walls, pressed at the narrow front between the ditches, and the English knights began to be killed by the advancing spear-points. The leading knights tried to retreat through the rest of the army, and soon all the English force was fleeing in disorder. Now Robert had a victory, and as a successful king he could gather allies.

King Edward had not finished dying when he heard the news of the defeat at Loudon Hill. He was outraged at Pembroke's inability to bring the fugitive Bruce to heel, and he climbed from his mobile deathbed onto his horse, donated the litter to the local cathedral and prepared to ride to Scotland. Four days later he had covered only the six miles to Burgh-on-Sands, and there he finally gave up his hunt for Robert Bruce and his hold on life, and so Edward Plantagenet died. His son completed the final Scottish campaign of his father by withdrawing his army after a token foray to the Scottish border.

At the end of 1307, with his English arch-enemy dead, Robert Bruce set about attacking his Scottish enemies. This was the third phase of the so-called Wars of Scottish Independence, running from the Bruce's coronation in 1306 to the Stirling Campaign of 1314. In these years of guerrilla warfare, every victory brought more followers. He battled more than jealousy and resentment of his killing of the Red Comyn; remember that when a nobleman threw in his lot with the Bruce, he gave up his English lands and connections. Some enemies Robert made peace with, some he defeated. The Earl of Ross was persuaded to keep his hands to himself for a time, long enough for Bruce to defeat more enemies and make Ross into an ally. Bruce fought the Earl of Buchan while propped upright in his saddle, right out of his sickbed. He sent his brother Edward, now made lord of Galloway and soon to be made Earl of Carrick, to commit the 'Harrowing of Buchan', a mass destruction and resettlement of Comyn lands, while the Earl of Buchan fled to England. In July 1308, the North Sea port city of Aberdeen was seized by the Bruce, opening to him the possibility of trade and alliance with both Norway (where his sister was dowager queen) and the Continent.

King Robert sent the Black Douglas, who had been his friend and ally since his coronation, to his home ground in the central Lowlands, there to harry the English. The Black Douglas was a friendly fellow and good fighter to his friends, but to his enemies his black hair and dark imagination made him a figure of terror. When Thomas Randolph, who had been captured by the English at Methven, was recaptured by the Black Douglas, he was antipathetic to the Bruce cause and especially displeased with the Bruce's methods of ungentlemanly guerrilla warfare. After only a few months spent with the charming Douglas, Randolph was a loyal follower of the Bruce.

The Black Douglas was a bogeyman to many people in Scotland and the north of England. The story is told of the Black Douglas sneaking into a castle, and overhearing a mother tell her child to go to sleep like a good bairn or the Black Douglas would come and get him. With a flourish he identified himself to the woman, and he spared her when he took the castle.

In 1309, three years of hard fighting since his coronation, King Robert summoned a parliament. The parliament not only confirmed the kingship of Scotland for King Robert, but confirmed the claim of his grandfather Robert the Competitor to the throne over the claims of the old Black Comyn and Toom Tabard. King Edward II, none too secure with his own barons, was easily convinced by his father-in-law, the king of France, to make peace with his Scottish neighbour.

King Robert used this leisure to cement the friendships he had made over his years of struggle, to establish a trade with

Ireland for English armaments and to establish a continental trade in spite of the English navy, such as it was. When Pope Clement in Avignon was influenced by his English friends (and by the cordial relations between a weak English king and France) to excommunicate King Robert on grounds of his breaking his oath of fealty to Edward I, the Scottish Church smoothed the problem over with their congregations. Here the Scottish Church was repaying King Robert for espousing their independence from York.

Late in 1310, King Edward sent an expedition against King Robert, but Robert avoided open combat and merely harassed the English army, especially on their withdrawal at the end of the campaigning season. Bruce proceeded to play a game of bluff and counter-bluff with King Edward, decoying English ships with leaked reports of Scottish naval operations and delaying the English king with offers of truces. When the English king was distracted by his own rebellious barons, Scottish armies poured over the border into England to demand blackmail. The Scottish protection racket extended as far south as the city of Durham, whose palatine bishop had always been the English king's strong arm in the north.

The Bruce followed a policy within Scotland of besieging the English castles. Apparently on the advice of the Black Douglas, he took the castles not by starvation nor by siege engines but by sneaking in over the walls when possible. One by one the chain of English castles fell between 1310 and 1314, until only Stirling and the castles of Lothian (including Edinburgh) remained under English command.

As each castle fell, King Robert had it dismantled. This was a usual practice of kings when subjugating rebellious barons, but it seems a bit odd since it was a king of Scots subduing old Scottish royal forts. The Bruce had no troops to spare for garrison duties, however, nor did he wish to tie his troops to known locations. So long as his army was a ghost army, appearing when the king of England was away and disappearing whenever an English army came near, he could not be defeated in battle. On the other hand, he did not wish the English to easily re-establish their control, and while the castles were just piles of rubble, such reconstruction would require an immensely expensive campaign for the English king.

This policy seems to imitate the policy of the Mamelukes, another army mobile in nature, who destroyed most of the fortresses of the first three crusades in order to keep the Franks from returning easily. As an avid would-be crusader, the Bruce would have heard of the activities of the Mameluke sultans of Egypt, who had only just prised loose the last foothold of Outremer, the Latin states in the Holy Land, by taking the fortress-city of Acre in 1291.

Lothian was a special problem for everyone, since it was still in fealty to England. The Earl of Dunbar continued to fulfil his duties to the English king, which included punishing his subjects when they paid their blackmail. Now the folk of his county boiled with resentment against the blackmailing Scots, with as much anger for Dunbar's men who exacted English retribution. Soon the Lothian problem became a moot point. Roxburgh fell to a sneaky plan of the Black Douglas. Edinburgh fell to yet another sneaky plan. For everyone save Dunbar, the problem was solved: the Earl of Dunbar's writ no longer ran beyond the walls of Dunbar Castle.

By the time the campaign season of 1314 began, none of the English castles in Scotland save Berwick, Jedburgh,

Dunbar and Stirling were left standing. All the others were rubble, the last debris of English occupation. When he assembled his army in the Tor Wood that May of 1314, Robert the Bruce had gone from being a lap-dog of the Plantagenet, to being the fugitive king of the isle of Rathlin, to being lord of Scotland north of the Tweed, allied with the Lord of the Isles and with the Earl of Ulster.

The picture which emerges of Robert Bruce is that of a man of almost preternatural determination. Yet there is another feature of his personality that is submerged under the mythic picture of the clenched jaw and hard eye: the sense of humour. To survive the years of wandering in the wilderness, Robert's personality must have been buoyant indeed. The friendship between him and the Black Douglas, a man known for his charm and humour, might well have been a cheerful association of two jolly men, looking at their reverses as opportunities for further adventure. It is rare in the extreme that a medieval king is known for his humour – jollity in statesmen is disapproved of even today – but if ever a king needed a sense of humour it was King Robert Bruce.

Robert the Bruce ended his days without ever fulfilling his dream of going on crusade. As he lay dying of leprosy, he echoed the dying wish of his nemesis King Edward I. Take my heart to the Holy Land, he begged the Black Douglas. Even if I should not live to go on crusade, my heart may fulfil my vow for me. Then, in 1329, King Robert I the Bruce of Scotland died aged fifty-four. The Black Douglas died in battle against the Muslim king of Granada at Zebas de Ardales in Spain, and the heart of Robert Bruce was buried in Melrose Abbey in Scotland.

4

The English Army

Information and Planning

Philip Mowbray reported to King Edward that Stirling would fall on St John's Day 1314 unless relieved by an English army. King Edward could expect that King Robert would oppose the relief. It was just this opposition that King Edward sought. He would summon an army, and march it to Stirling. If the king of Scots did not oppose him, he would relieve the garrison at Stirling Castle, and use the fortress as a base to re-establish his castles north of the Forth. If the king of Scots still did not oppose him, the king of England would end the campaign season with his chain of fortresses renewed, the faith of his Scottish followers restored and Robert Bruce back where he started: ruler of nothing much. If at any time King Robert attempted an open battle, he could be defeated on the field. If, as was more likely, King Robert attempted to conduct his usual campaign of guerrilla warfare, harrying the English army and running away, King Edward had a little surprise for him.

King Edward Longshanks, through some very clever generals, had turned Wales from a wild jungle of untamed tribal chiefs into a heavily garrisoned, tightly controlled province.

Wales, divided into sections, was ruled by a committee of English nobles, whose royal appointments gave them revenues and privileges. These lords, the marcher lords, had within their provinces hordes of soldiers, trained in intertribal conflict and in the incessant wars with the English. The Welsh were especially known for providing knifemen, soldiers trained in nothing but stabbing fallen foes. In ordinary battles, with cavalry and billmen, these soldiers were not terribly effective. Chroniclers of the Battle of Falkirk compete with one another in deriding the usefulness of the Welsh, accusing them of being either useless or traitorous, defecting to the Scots. King Edward had a new use for them: his little surprise for the Bruce.

Word came from English friends in Scotland that the Scottish army would be mustering just outside Stirling. Veterans of the many battles and sieges near Stirling knew that the area to the north and west of the castle was mountainous, and that the area to the east and south-east was a swamp. Expecting the Bruce to take refuge in the bogs and hills, he would use his Welsh foot soldiers like hounds to chase after him there. Just as Edward I had turned the humble English archer into a formidable fighting arm, Edward II planned to turn the humble Welsh knifeman into a force to be feared. They would fight the Scottish foot soldiers in the bogs, where horse and pike were useless. They would overwhelm the Scots with numbers, and defeat the sneaky Bruce at his own game. If Bruce fled into the wooded hills, as was his wont, there would be a vast supply of vicious Welshmen to chase him down. For this purpose, King Edward summoned 21,000 foot soldiers, including billmen as well as archers and knifemen. He did not expect all he summoned to come, but if even a good proportion of the summoned foot soldiers came to the rendezvous at Wark there would be a formidable army of hounds to hunt down the Scottish fox.

King Edward was prepared for a major campaign against the Bruce, with a navy scheduled to sail from East Anglian and Welsh ports against Argyll and the Isles. They would land an Irish army in Argyll, and attempt to recruit men there to fight the Bruce's friend, the Lord of the Isles, to keep the Bruce from melting away into the protection of the Islemen, where he had been so safe just after his coronation. The summer of 1314 would not just see the relief of Stirling, but the complete destruction of Robert Bruce as an enemy, and with him the dreams of an independent Scottish kingdom. To accomplish this, King Edward was prepared to bet the farm.

Paying for the Army

Economics does not generally make its way into the popular idea of medieval armies. The reality is, however, that an army was a great, unproductive horde of men that positively consumed resources. Not only did the soldiers cease to be productive farm labourers as soon as they were called up, and persist in eating and drinking a great deal in spite of the fact that they were no longer productive, with their fields left to rack and ruin, but they actually demanded cash money in return for their services. Ordinary Englishmen asked to leave their counties to fight as foot soldiers were paid about 2d *per diem*. Knights not on their feudal service were paid about 4s *per diem*.

Even discounting the economic costs of war in crops lost etc, an army was expensive. The cost of an army consisted of paying the troops, contracting for sutlers to sell them food, contracting teamsters to transport the sutlers' goods and other military hardware, and various ancillary expenses. Food for the warhorses needed to be bought at about 6d per animal *per diem*, making a horse more expensive than a private soldier. Tradesmen would have to be hired, such as armourers, farriers (blacksmiths who specialised in horses), sappers (who specialised in digging holes and tunnels and in building bridges) and others. When the war was done, the king would need to reimburse knights whose expensive horses were killed on the campaign.

The problem of military pay was a bugbear of warlike English kings since the days of Magna Carta, when the English barons impressed upon King John that they preferred to be asked before taxes in excess of feudal duties could be levied. Only a few years before, King Edward had conceded that he could only set the prices for military supplies in consultation with a parliament. The Ordinances had put King Edward in an especially tough position, since they had banished the king's banker, Amerigo Frescobaldi. Unlike Longshanks, who could rely on copious credit from the House of Frescobaldi (the king of England could always provide a county or two as collateral, though it was sometimes hard to collect in the event of default), Edward II, forced to resort to representatives of other banking houses, could not as easily borrow large sums of money. The result was that he could not raise an army unless he either paid for it from his own purse (and line of credit), provisioning it at market prices, or summoned a parliament of his nobles and convinced them to pay for it.

King Edward's only remaining recourse was to levy his feudal host. This was an army in which anyone who owned land was required to participate for forty days and nights without pay. The army was drawn from the nobles themselves, the knights whom they employed, and the tenants of their lands, but its numbers and composition were only vaguely fixed in the Assizes of Arms, issued first by Henry II and re-issued by Longshanks in 1285. The basis for the levy was that England consisted of just over 6,278 knight's fees, that is parcels of land large enough to support a knight and his official and private families for a year. For every knight's fee a man or woman owned, he was responsible for providing one knight or two lesser horsemen to serve in the king's host. A catch-22 of this system of obligations was this: the more powerful the feudal magnate was, and the more useful he would be in war, the more capable he was of baldly underestimating the number of knight's fees he owned. Thus the barons with the most money and with the largest numbers of followers were both the most desirable and the hardest to summon of the feudal levy. An example of the response is the levy of 1310, when the Earl of Lancaster responded to the summons of the feudal levy for service in Scotland. Lancaster, who was also Earl of Leicester, Derby, Lincoln and Salisbury, was tired of being called 'Play-Actor' by Piers Gaveston. So the largest landowner in England besides the king estimated that his lands were worth only six knights' fees and offered four knights and four lesser horsemen as his entire obligation to the feudal levy.

Levying the king's host was not only a matter of gathering an army. Since not every owner of property or money could fight (women, underage and elderly noblemen, merchants and abbots, for instance), the paying of shield-money –'scutage' in Law French – was an acceptable alternative. The theory is that non-combatants pay enough to provide a substitute knight for each knight's fee owned. In years of relative peace, when military expenses were primarily those of garrisoning castles, the 'levying' of the host was just one more tax. Even when the host was really raised, care was generally taken to make it self-financing by raising only a portion as troops, and using the scutage from the rest to pay the expenses. In years of peace, powerful nobles like Lancaster could get away with paying correspondingly less scutage.

The feudal levy was not large enough to provide an army for war. It was generally better policy for an English king to summon an entire host as scutage rather than as troops, and use the money to pay and equip an army, raising the remainder of the funds from other sources. This bought the king an army of willing cavalry soldiers who knew that they would be paid in good silver, rather than an army of resentful knights who did their feudal duty grudgingly.

The last source of support for the king in time of war came from those who relied on the king's support. Some nobles' interests were closely tied to the king's, and these nobles were bound to turn out their levies and open their treasuries in support of the king their sponsor. Included in this category were the king's relatives and those nobles such as the marcher lords whose appointments depended on royal favour.

A popular king, or a king about to conduct a popular war, could rely on a parliament of his peers to approve purveyance and funding for raising an army and sending it on campaign. A rich king could hire the army out of his own pocket. In the event, Edward II was so unpopular among his barons that to summon a parliament would have been to bring together a great conference of his enemies. His own pocket was deep

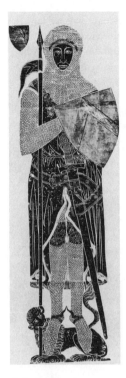  

Left to right:

1 Brass of Sir J. D'Aubernoun, Stoke Dabernon, Surrey, 1277. The profile of Sir John's head shows that he is wearing a bascinet beneath his mail coif. The gigue strap from his shield is clearly visible on his right shoulder. The shortened depiction of his lance shows his arms on a pointed pennon, indicating that he was a knight but not a knight banneret, whose lance would have a square banner.

2 Brass of Sir R. de Trumpington, Trumpington, Cambridgeshire, 1289.

3 Brass of Sir R. de Bures, Acton, Suffolk, 1302.

Left: 4 Brass of Sir Robert de Setvans, or Septefans, in a 1306 brass from Chartham, Kent. Sir Robert's mailcoif and ailettes have been thrown back from his shoulders to show us his long hair (which would have provided padding under the coif). Similarly his mail mittens are left hanging to reveal his hands. A scolloped fabric pad keeps his mail shirt from rattling on his wrought-iron knee cops. His shield is painted with three wickerwork fans, a pun on his surname.

Below left: 5 John Balliol from a Scottish Armorial illuminated between 1581 and 1584.

Below right: 6 King Robert Bruce and his second wife form a Scottish Armorial of the reign of Queen Mary, illuminated between 1561 and 1565.

Right: 7 Seal of Robert Bruce, Earl of Carrick.

Far right: 8 The tomb of Angus Og MacDonald. A good friend of Robert Bruce, Angus Og was with him at Bannockburn.

Below: 9 Letters patent of John Balliol dated at Newcastle-Upon-Tyne, 24 December 1292, recording that he had sworn fealty to Edward.

Left: 10 Great seal of Robert I (1306-29), showing the king crowned and enthroned in state. The seal is modelled deliberately on that of his predecessors, especially Alexander III, to stress the legitimacy of his succession.

Middle: 11 Great seal of Robert I (1306-29), showing the king as a mounted and armoured knight. The symbolism is appropriate for a king who ruled at the head of a military regime and whose power rested on control of the military resources of Scotland.

Below left: 12 Scottish foot soldier of the late thirteenth century, as depicted in the margin of an English manuscript. It was infantry such as this, unarmoured and carrying short-sword and spears, who comprised the bulk of the Scottish armies at Stirling Bridge, Falkirk and Bannockburn.

Right: 13 Silver penny of Robert I. Ransoms and the plunder and 'protection money' offered by the northern English counties brought a great influx of bullion to Scotland, especially after 1314.

Above: 14 The Tower of London in the seventeenth century.

Left: 15 A sixteenth-century depiction of the parliament supposedly held in the 1270s, with Alexander III and Llewelyn, Prince of Wales, sitting at the feet of Edward I.

16 King Edward II's elaborate tomb, Gloucester Cathedral, *c.*1665.

Above left: 17 Edward III.

Above right: 18 Hugh Despenser the Younger, from a window in the clerestory of Tewkesbury Abbey, *c.*1334.

Left: 19 Arms on the tomb of Sir James Douglas in St Bride's. Sir James was killed in Spain on the way to take the heart of Robert the Bruce to the Holy Land.

Right: 20 The arms of some of Scotland's powerful nobles: Dunbar, Earl of March; Randolph, Earl of Moray; Douglas, Earl of Douglas; Douglas, Earl of Angus.

Below: 21 Seal of John Balliol.

Above: 22 Edward I, as depicted on his seal of 1276.

Above: 23 The royal coat of arms of Edward II: 'the leopards of Anjou'.

Right: 24 King Edward II as a weeper at the tomb of John of Eltham. These carved figures on tombs represented relatives of the deceased.

Clockwise from top left:

25 The paternal arms of Robert the Bruce when he was Bruce of Annandale, before his coronation.

26 The heraldic arms of Scotland, 'the lion rampant within a double tressure fleury-counter-fleury' – a beast surrounded by a fence of spear-points.

27 Coat of arms of Ingraham de Umfraville, whose lands in Carrick were restored by Edward Longshanks 'on his deathbed'.

28 Seventeenth-century engraving of Robert the Bruce, commemorating his coronation in 1306.

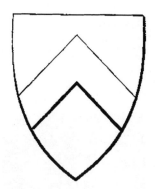

Clockwise from above left:

29 The arms of Sir Edward Bruce, Robert's brother and sometime Earl of Carrick.

30, 31 The coats of arms of Thomas Randolph of Strathdon, Earl of Moray, and Sir James Douglas, 'the Black Douglas'. The Earl of Moray beecame regent of Scotland after the Bruce's death in 1329.

32 A King Edward halfpenny (left) and penny, such as would have been used to pay for the the men and provisions necessary for a military campaign.

Left: 33 Brass from the tomb of Robert the Bruce, Dunfermline Abbey.

Right: 34 Carving of a thirteenth-century knight, Furness Abbey.

enough to finance some of the expedition, and some credit might have been found in Italian banking houses, but to have bought an army of mercenaries (especially foreign mercenaries) would only have further inflamed his own nobles against him. So the king summoned the feudal host of England as well as large levies from Wales and the Welsh marches, which levies would come cheaply. The feudal host that came to the muster at Wark-on-Tweed was a shadow of the army summoned. Of the English earls only three personally answered the summons, all relatives of the king by blood or marriage. The rest only sent the bare minimum of men that they estimated they owed under the Assize of Arms. The marcher lords brought their Welsh knifemen, the northern sheriffs brought the men of their counties, and the king's friends brought their men.

Transport and Supply

The chronicler Froissart tells of a campaign against the Scots in the north of England conducted by Edward III early in his career. Throughout the campaign, as they advanced northwards, the English attempted to live off the country, and failed miserably. The Scots poached the king's deer and rustled local cattle, driving herds away from the English army, while purveyors all along the route sold food to the English sutlers at ruinous prices. When he planned his Scottish campaign of 1314, Edward II did not make the same mistake as his son would, and as he himself had before: he planned for his army to be supplied along its route.

An army needs a wide range of commodities in order to function in the field. The most basic, water, is in plentiful supply in Britain. Food is plentiful in various forms through-out the island, but since it does not just fall from the sky, its owners tend to be less generous with it than they can be with water. Thus one must either steal food from the own-ers (which is easy to do if one is a crowd of several hundred armed men), buy it in bulk and transport it with the army by wagon or use the wagons to carry money and buy provisions along the way. In practice, provisioning was a combination of the three. Money had to be transported in any case, since those troops and servants who were not part of the feudal levy had to be paid.

English roads had not been systematically maintained since the Romans abandoned Britain almost a thousand years before. In a thousand years, roads can fall into a very sad state of repair indeed. Thus, except in those parishes that had taken special care to maintain the Roman roads, it was very difficult to move goods overland.

One aspect of transport that the king of England had some control over, however, was shipping by sea. For an island nation, transport of goods by water is important. Due to the agrarian nature of the feudal political system, ports and shipping were not under the control of land barons, but under control of the citizens of the port towns. These towns relied on royal protection from the encroachment of feudal magnates, and often paid well in cash for this protection. Now the king demanded another sort of payment. The port towns of England, from Weymouth in the west to Wark in the north, would provide ships to provision the army. The Scottish Rolls list twenty-eight captains and their ships to be used in this operation, with captains John Sturmy and Peter Bard as admirals of the fleet.

This fleet did not include those ships which had been dispatched under letters of marque to harass Scottish trade, and to try to stop the flow to Scotland of munitions from Ireland, Flanders and Norway. Neither did this fleet include the ships provided to the earls, at their own expense, for the shipping of their copious personal goods to Scotland. Yet another fleet seems to have been raised in East Anglia and Wales under the command of one John of Argyll, which was intended to recruit allies in Argyll and the Isles to turn them and 4,000 Irish marines against the Bruce.

The soldiers would be summoned to Wark-on-Tweed. The knights were protected on their way by warrants of safe-conduct issued by the king, which proved that they were not marching armies to attack the lands of the nobles along the way. Until they got to Wark, their overlords were responsible for their care and feeding. Although this was expensive for the marcher lords, who had to march their men across the breadth of England, food could be bought along the way. Once they were at the rendezvous, they could be supplied by ships anchored in the River Tweed. When the army moved north through Lauderdale, the supply ships would sail ahead to meet them at Edinburgh on the Firth of Forth. When the army moved on to Stirling, the ships would sail up the River Forth and re-supply the army as well as the garrison of the castle there.

This system of seagoing replenishment meant that on each leg of the journey the army only needed to bring with it enough to take it to its next port. Thus the number of wagons needed to trundle over the ancient roads was kept to a minimum. The number of wagons was still very large. Financed from royal revenues, an armada of wagons was raised and sent to the army's staging ground at Berwick. Wagons were scheduled to arrive continuously throughout the summer, to supply the campaign against the Scottish army in the hills and forests as well as to supply the rebuilding of English fortresses.

The cost of transporting goods by wagon increases exponentially with the size of the army. Each wagon was pulled by four horses or eight oxen, and each beast required a combination of grazing and fodder in order to keep it going. The horses consumed primarily hay, oats, beans and pease, all bulky goods. With each additional wagon came additional draught beasts, and an additional weight of fodder had to be dragged along as well. Entire wagons were given over to transporting food for the other pack animals. This was in addition to the fodder needed by the warhorses and the troops' riding mounts. Eventually a supply train reaches a point of limited returns, at which adding a wagon and its team does not add significantly to the amount of available haulage.

Oxen were yoked in pairs, and were herded along by drovers. The ox's musculature allows the strain of pulling a load to be taken on the beast's humped shoulders with a simple yoke. The horses for each wagon wore horse collars, distributing the load over their chests and shoulders, and were tied with rope traces in single file. The single file of loosely tied horses was difficult to control, and required postilions riding some of the horses: yet more manpower. Carthorses also required regular shoeing, thus more farriers to do the work and stocks of iron weighing down more wagons. The carts also needed technicians in case they required repair: skilled wainwrights and wheelwrights who needed to be fed and paid more than common soldiers.

Lest anyone think that the difficulty of transport reduced the wealthy knights and earls to sleeping rough, remember that the personal possessions and provisions of the Earl of Hereford merited their own entire ship. King Edward organised a travelling wine cellar to be established at Newcastle, acting as an oenal staging base for the expedition. The English nobility was making this trip in style.

The Knights

I use the term 'knight' loosely here to refer to those who showed up for military service with the arms and appurtenances of a knight. Many of these had not gone to the trouble and expense of being dubbed knights, and were thus classified as lesser horsemen. These men-at-arms were probably not as keenly interested in war as their dubbed comrades, and were not as likely to trouble themselves with the state of the art in arms, equipment and horses. They were certainly considered by the knights who ran the military show to be a lesser sort, and their military value was considered to be less. For the purposes of this discussion, however, the men who fought in full armour with lances on big horses are knights.

The knights expected their participation in any military engagement to consist of an heroic charge against the enemy knights in which many would be unhorsed and killed. They conceived that victory in this charge would go to the knight with the better equipment and horse, but more importantly the victor would be the fiercer and more skilled knight. Note that the knight compared himself to the single opponent whom he would attack, rather than seeing his battalion and the opposing battalion as tactical units in the battle. When the dust cleared, the unhorsed knights would be ransomed, the dead would be sent home to honourable burial and the victors would thank God for their victory.

Any other features of the battle, like tactics or use of archery and infantry, were not chivalrous, and thus somewhat suspect. The fact that English participation in the Welsh wars consisted of useless chivalrous combat and successful co-ordinated action was probably lost on most English knights. If one were to approach a knight on the eve of battle in the late thirteenth or early fourteenth century, and ask him what he was going to do the next day, he would answer that he was going to charge gloriously and through his own fierceness and skill and piety unhorse at least one opponent, possibly several. This does not, however, mean that he would do this the next day. He would just as likely charge archers or other peasant foot soldiers, sending them scurrying for cover while his own side's archers won the battle for him.

Equipment

The main military appurtenances of the medieval knight were armour, weapons and horses. These were often given to knights on their being dubbed, and this has to do with more than ceremony. All of these were very expensive, and a knight needed either to own enough land to afford the equipment, to be employed by someone who did, or to make enough money as a professional soldier (or in some other profession, in the case of a lesser horseman) to keep himself equipped. One way or another, every Englishman who owned land worth more than £15 or goods worth more than 40 marks (£26 13s 7d) was required by the Assizes of Arms to own the basic equipment of the heavy horseman.

The main weapon of the medieval knight was the sword. A sword is, at its simplest, a long diamond-shaped prism consisting of a bar of steel shaped into two wedges. The user holds the end of the prism by the grip and attempts to use his own main strength, applied through the wedges, to hack his opponent into immobility and death. The main problem of the sword is that in order to make it hard enough to cause damage (rather than bend) and hold an edge without being brittle enough to break on impact requires the work of a highly skilled blacksmith. The smith must carefully forge the blade by adding just the right amount of carbon to the iron, then temper and anneal the blade to just the right hardness. Especially skilful smiths – such as those expert in the 'damascus' method and other techniques of welding pieces of differently tempered steel – commanded high fees indeed, and even the simplest sword was expensive. This expense is reflected in the fact that only the richest soldiers, the knights, could afford to fight with swords.

The value of a sword is also reflected in the almost religious status it gains in chivalric romances of the Middle Ages. Only a few people know the name of King Arthur's spear, since it is rarely mentioned in legend (according to Geoffrey of Monmouth the spear was called Ron). His sword Excalibur (or Caliburn) and its special properties, as well as the sword he drew from the stone, are all strong features of chivalric legend. The special mystique of the sword is also reflected in the general myths about the production of swords. One famous legend is that damascus swords were tempered by being thrust through the (temporarily) living body of a slave, instead of the usual bath of salt water. This might reflect very powerful marketing techniques by the makers of damascus steel, if the rumour was created deliberately (perhaps in a demonstration). This procedure might, on the other hand, have actually been followed, reflecting a triumph of form over substance. While the human abdomen is a dramatic tempering bath, its variation in salinity, temperature and acidity make it a poor one indeed. This myth definitely reflects an awe of the best swords that continued long after serviceable blades had become commonplace.

The more workaday tool of the knight was the lance. A lance is a spear adapted to use from horseback. It consists, like most spears, of a wooden shaft with a metal point on the end. The point of the lance was the traditional leaf-shaped spear point, an ancient form of blade that is especially effective at cutting through armour. Lighter lances were designed to be used as stabbing weapons held at arm's length. The Bayeux Tapestry carries illustrations of Norman knights, two hundred years before Bannockburn, fighting with such lances.

Heavier lances were designed to be used 'couched', that is held tightly under the arm, pointing forward. If a knight had only his hand to hold the lance, as the Normans did at Hastings, a couched charge would likely result in the knight losing his grip on impact. Lances depicted in illustrations from the early 1300s seem to have no device for stopping the lance: it was held in place by main force of hand and arm, and clasped tightly to the ribcage. Later solutions included a stop that transmitted impact to the knight's shield, and a metal cuff (often mistaken for a hand-guard) that rested against the knight's shoulder and chest so that on impact the lance would be braced against the knight's body. The hand held the lance up to the armpit, fixing it firmly with the shaft of the lance pointing to the left across the horse's neck, resting on the shield. His lance could be controlled only within a tight circle. Any other aiming he could do he did by aiming his horse. The couched lance integrated the horseman, the horse and the lance into one unit, and the unit was sent charging, like a bullet from a gun, in one direction.

The knight rode his horse in a tall military saddle (the ancestor of the American western saddle), with a high bow in front of him and a high cantle at his back. He began his charge with the lance upright and resting on a saddle attachment. As he charged he leaned forward with his hindquarters planted against the cantle. Thus the shock of impact was transferred from his shoulder and chest to his buttocks to the horse, instead of propelling him off the horse's rear or hitting his lower back against the cantle. He sat with his knees locked at full extension, almost standing. This was so that lateral impacts would not send him flying off sideways, and more importantly so that when he used his sword he would have secure footing. The result was a stable three-point stance (two stirrups and the cantle) for fighting. As he neared impact the knight took his lance from its rest on the saddle, and lowered it into position, pointing towards the foe.

The horse was controlled by a curb bit, an especially vicious piece of equipment. Not only does a curb bit put a horse into a foul, fierce mood, it lets the horse know on no uncertain terms how he is being steered. The bit was attached to reins held by the knight in his shield hand. To try to turn his horse he swung his entire shield, and with it the horse's head.

Besides sword and lance, the remaining weapons at the knight's disposal were workaday tools, without the cachet of the sword. They included maces and axes specialised to work against certain types of armour. The knight might also have a dagger, as well as a short, crude meat-cleaver of a sword called a falchion. It must be emphasised that there was no standard kit for a knight. Even types of armour varied widely from one knight to the next, with hand-me-down daggers and used-armour purchases making each knight's equipment clearly his own.

The knight's horse was also a specialised piece of equipment, since the sort of horse suited to pulling a cart or plough is different from a warhorse. In Great Britain especially, horses large enough to run quickly while carrying an armoured man were scarce. Breeding stock needed to be continually imported from France and especially from Spain, and a good warhorse cost as much as £30 or more each (150 days pay at a dubbed knight's 4s *per diem*). Even the largest 'destriers', as these warhorses were called, were not large by modern standards of horseflesh, and it is generally accepted that the proportions in period illustrations, with the men almost dwarfing the horses, are a reflection of actual proportions rather than being merely poor renderings.

Desirable in a destrier were thick, short legs, a broad chest, an arched neck and a broad back. Small heads and ears were considered especially impressive, and contemporary illustrations occasionally flatter knights by showing them on pin-headed horses with necks curved in a complete circle. Flattering illustrations of warhorses are also careful to give them vicious facial expressions, making it clear that the horses are not only well-formed but fierce as well. The destrier was 15 or 16 hands high (a hand is 10cm or 4in, and horses are measured from ground to withers), as compared to the modern beer-wagon horse which measures 17-18 hands. Stallions were preferred over mares or geldings to the point of exclusion.

The writer Tim Severin, famous for building and sailing reconstructions of ancient vessels, attempted to ride a European Great Horse (the sort of destriers that English earls imported and bred at great expense) from France to Jerusalem. By the time he got to Hungary, the gait and wide back of the huge Belgian had caused him a great deal of pain and fatigue. Severin was forced to acquire a lighter horse for riding, and lead the destrier behind, carrying the luggage.

This is not surprising, considering that medieval knights routinely rode smaller horses called 'palfreys' and saved their larger horses for battle. While it has been assumed that this was to keep the warhorses fresh for combat, it is certain that this was done for reasons of comfort as well. The palfrey was, in fact, a 'pacing' horse, that is it strode with both right legs and both left legs moving in unison, making for a very smooth ride.

The horseshoes used on destriers were different from those for palfreys, but similar to those used for draught horses. They were forged with cleats on the bottom for better gripping in soft ground. One illustration shows horseshoes made wider than the hoof, with cleats protruding upward from the rim, probably to protect the horse's hooves from damaging each other in the confusing motions of close combat.

A dubbed knight was expected to have at least one destrier and two palfreys, as well as one or two horses called 'rounceys', which were some sort of cheaper horse, ridden as a warhorse by squires and other lesser horsemen. Two or three extra in each category was not uncommon.

Horses could be padded to protect them from spears and arrows. The chest and face especially would be protected.

Great cloth trappers might be used as well, to catch and turn weapons. The heaviest destriers were strong enough not only to carry an armoured knight, but some of their own metal armour as well. Most horses carried 'barding' consisting of cloth padding and hardened leather deflecting surfaces.

The basic armour of the knights at Bannockburn was mail. Mail, or chain mail as it is also known, is a mesh made of interlocking rings. Modern butchers use it to protect their hands from the edges of their sharp knives, and medieval knights used it primarily to protect themselves from the edges of their opponents' swords. Mail is made by first making small iron rings, either by forging them from iron rod or cutting them from wire. The rings are made with their ends as overlapping flat sections. The flat sections are pierced with a punch. Then half of the rings are closed, each with a tiny rivet. Four riveted links are hung on one open link, which is then riveted shut. These clusters of five rings are then joined together with more open rings, which must then be riveted shut. This is a very time-consuming process, which required a very skilled smith, resulting in a costly piece of armour, at a minimum of £1 (5 to 10 days' wages for a dubbed knight) for the equipment, including helmet.

Chain mail is good protection from a sharp edge, and its flexibility allows the wearer to fight effectively. The very same flexibility, however, makes it poor protection against the weight of a weapon; for example, bones can be broken through chain mail. To augment the chain mail, the knight wore a thickly padded coat underneath. Called a gambeson, pourpoint or jack, this coat was several inches thick, faced on the outside with canvas or leather, and padded with wool, tow or hair. This padding not only absorbed the force of a sword's impact, it also caused the chain mail to hang away from the wearer's body, forcing the sword's wielder to move a heavy piece of iron mail with his weapon and thus slowing it down.

The mace and the falchion were weapons designed to negate the protective effect of chain mail. These weapons, the former like a sledgehammer and the latter like a meat cleaver, were designed with the main weight of the weapon far from the user's hand, towards the tip. This made the mace's head or the falchion's point swing with a great deal more force than a sword. Although this made these weapons more difficult to manage, it helped to move the weight of the mail and to compress the padding of the gambeson. The mace was designed to cause massive haemorrhages, to destroy muscles and to break bones. The falchion was designed to cleave through the mail while causing the same sorts of injury, with laceration as an added hazard. Neither of these was especially difficult to make, and the falchion and the mace were not treated with the same reverence as the proper sword, though the mace had a ceremonial function as the symbol of a constable's office.

There are parts of the body that are not meant to bend, which therefore gain nothing from the flexibility of chain mail, and can benefit from more rigid protection. The four-teenth-century knight covered these places with plates of wrought iron, either in addition to or instead of mail. The first part of the body to be covered in rigid armour was the head, covered by a helmet since ancient times. The next parts to be covered with plate are those bones which, like the skull, do not have a covering of flesh to protect them from break-ing. The outsides of the knees and elbows, the tops of the shoulders and the fronts of the shins were prime candidates to be protected from crushing force. A crushing blow to the thigh might cause a nasty bruise, while the same blow to the shin would break it easily. A few hard blows to the elbows and knees through the course of a knight's working life could result in long-term disability. The chest was often covered by a plastron made of iron, but it seems to have been worn under the chain mail. Hence the part-mail and part-plate armour characteristic of the early fourteenth century.

Plates called 'ailettes' were affixed to the shoulders. Many scholars assume that these were to protect the shoulders, another delicate joint. Their vertical position and loose mounting, however, provides little protection from a sword cutting downward. It is more likely that the ailette was designed to protect the neck from lateral lance and sword blows by turning the weapon aside. The ailette also served to help identify the knight, emblazoned as it often was with his coat of arms. The other piece of neck protection was the gorget, a metal collar worn by those willing to sacrifice a bit of flexibility in order to keep head and body together.

Sometimes the use of plates extended over the abdomen of the fighter. These plates, riveted into a leather or cloth jacket, either covered or replaced sections of the mail shirt. They provided more protection against crushing blows to the abdomen, at the expense of flexibility. An additional advantage to these 'coats of plates' was that it was cheaper to pay a smith to make plates of wrought iron than to have him engage in the laborious process of riveting mail. In addition, the relatively thin pieces of metal used in these coats were significantly lighter than the thick, redundant mass of mail. Similar use of small plates was sometimes made in hand armour, covering the knight's mail mittens with iron plates to protect the small bones of the hand.

The helmet had seen some interesting development since the conical hats worn by William the Bastard and his colleagues in the Bayeux Tapestry. The Normans and their English opponents wore steel caps with a 'nasal', that is a metal extension over the nose which protected the face from injury. Beneath these caps was a coif of mail, with a bib that tied across the wearer's face. The coif was fitted over padding and a curious haircut to cushion the head. In the twelfth century, as the couched-lance style of fighting became popular with knights, the 'great helm' or 'barrel helm' gained popularity. This was a wrought-iron barrel with slots for vision and holes for breathing, and its cylindrical form presented a rounded glancing surface for lances. It was worn over a round steel cap called a 'helmet' (little helm) or 'bascinet'. A mail coif might be worn under the bascinet, or a version of the coif called an aventail might be attached like a skirt to the edges of the bascinet.

At first knights wore their great helms both for tournaments and for war, covering the barrels with cloth mantlings while on crusade in tropical climes. During the fourteenth century, knights began to set aside the protection of the great helm for the sake of mobility and visibility. Although they always wore their great helms in tournament, they began to ride on the field of battle in their bascinets and aventails, foregoing some degree of protection in favour of visibility and easy breathing. This might indicate a shifting of emphasis from fighting other knights with couched lance to charging only against infantry, and fighting knights at close range with swords. Bascinets began to be fitted with rounded or conical visors to present a safe, curved surface to a lance-tip or arrow-head, but these visors were designed to be removed or to turn out of the way for visibility.

The shield served a dual purpose for the knight, providing protection as well as serving as the knight's surrogate face on the battlefield. Shields tended to be made of wood covered with leather. The shape of the shield is called a 'heater' by modern historians, since its shape is similar to the heating surface of a flatiron. They were curved both to present a good glancing surface to a lance as well as to improve their balance. The use of wood rather than metal shields had an advantage in sword combat: a sword tended to bite into the edge of a wooden shield, temporarily surrendering control of the blade to the shield's owner.

The leather face of the shield was painted with the knight's heraldic bearings, sometimes called a 'coat of arms'. This allowed the knight to be distinguished among many men all wearing similar fashionable helmets. Recognition was not only important to a knight's friends, so that they would not attack him in a mêlée, but to his enemies, so that they would not kill him but hold him for ransom should his shield identify him as someone of importance. The coat of arms, or motifs therefrom, could be repeated on the knights' coats, on their horses' trappings and on their servants' coats and trappings as well.

The knights were accompanied by squires and other mounted men-at-arms, in small units called 'lances'. Some squires were young men learning the ropes in preparation for being knighted, while others would never be wealthy or favoured enough to command their own lances. The classical number of a lance was three men: one knight, one squire and one lesser horseman, though greater men had greater numbers of squires. The purpose of the lesser horsemen was to protect their boss, to see him off the field if he was hurt and to help the heralds to negotiate ransom if he was captured.

The profession of herald was only then evolving. In the previous century heralds were a sort of minstrel who specialised in war, memorialising the valorous deeds of battle. This required them to be expert in telling one knight from the next in the thick of battle, and so they learned the coats of arms that the knights wore, and the symbols painted on their shields. By the beginning of the fourteenth century it became commonplace for heralds to draw or paint rolls of arms, which were books of the different coats that the knights wore. As the heralds evolved into a separate profession from the minstrels, they became specialists in the chivalric niceties of warfare, like ransom and surrender. Like guildsmen they chose their own masters, Kings of Arms like the Kings of Minstrels, and became a special sort of household servant.

When the English knight of 1314 was out of his fighting gear, he wore a woollen coat that was tailored to fit his body closely. Over this he wore an overcoat that had sleeves flaring at the elbow into hanging tippets. He wore tailored woollen stockings that tied to his under-coat, and gartered them below the knees. Under all this he wore small-clothes of linen or cotton. The knight's clothing had no pockets. He hung his pockets, or pouches, on a belt, and with them a dagger. His dagger, called a 'ballock' dagger, was shaped with a somewhat rude hilt. In 1314 the dagger was still worn nearly parallel to the belt; in later years young dandies would hang their ballock daggers over their groins as advertising.

The knight showed his wealth in the use of fancy fabrics, like silk, in place of wool, in embroidery and expensive decoration, in careful tailoring, and in expensive accessories. Outdoors the knight put on a loose-fitting woollen mantle that covered him to his knees, with slits to allow him to reach the equipment on his belt. He wore on his head a fitted hood, with a long tail called a liripipe. His hat might be tall and rounded with a narrow brim.

Archers

The English army mustered thousands of infantry. Many of these carried bills, knives and even swords. Many rode horses on their way to war, and many would even fight on horseback alongside their marching comrades. On the field by the Bannockburn, however, it was not the Welsh knifeman or the mounted archer or even the odd crossbowman who played a part, it was the Englishman with his bow.

The bow is, in its simplest form, a pair of levers which share a fulcrum. The fulcrum is the archer's hand at the centre of a single piece of wood. When the bow is held at the centre, and the ends drawn back by the bowstring, it is comparable to a lever with the fulcrum very close to one end. The torsion provided by the bending of the wood is comparable to a heavy weight on the short end of the lever. If one were to press down the long end of a lever, raising a heavy weight on the short end, and then release it, the long end of the lever would fly upward with great force and speed (any number of Road Runner cartoons can provide adequate demonstration of this principle). Just so, when the bowstring is released the ends of the bow swing rapidly forward until the string is taut, and the arrow held against the string is propelled with great force and speed. It seems unnecessary to explain a system so simple as a bow and arrow, but this extensive description is helpful in understanding the special features of the English long bow: its thickness and composition provided a great deal of torsion, and its great length provided leverage to bend the thick wood.

The long English bow was traditionally made from yew, though some other woods could be used. The straight trunk of the yew tree, a poisonous evergreen, was cut lengthwise into pieces about as long as a man was tall and 15cm (6in) around at the widest point. The bow was cut carefully from the tree-trunk so that its sapwood formed the springy outer layer and the heartwood formed the tough inner layer, producing the torsion that powers the bow. It was important to the bow's structural integrity that the grain of the wood run the entire length of the bow, and not transect the bow at any point. The string was made of hemp, the same fibre (cannabis) used in making canvas.

The bow was held at full extension of the left arm, with the right hand holding the centre of the string. The right hand was drawn to the cheekbone, and the archer sighted across the arrow's point. The archer wore a shield on the inside of his left forearm to protect his flesh from the impact of the bowstring as it brushed past, as well as a glove to protect the fingers that held the bowstring from being sliced like cheese on a wire.

A set of measurements set down in a court case of accessory to murder in 1298 tell us what the alleged murder weapon, a barbed arrow, was like. The arrow was three quarters of an ell long (an ell is about 114cm or 45in, thus the arrow was 86cm or 34in long) and 2.5cm (1in) thick. Feather 'fletches' tied to the shaft helped to stabilise the arrow in flight. This mighty weapon, which if the measurements are accurate is significantly heavier than a modern target arrow, was propelled by a longbow and penetrated about 16cm (6in) into the victim's thorax.

Momentum is defined as mass multiplied by velocity. The significant mass of such an arrow propelled at high speed from a powerful long bow and striking with the thin, sharp blade of the arrow head can do a great deal of damage. Shields can be penetrated, even the links of mail can be cut by the head. Some arrows were made with 'bodkin' points, that is points that were long and thin to penetrate the gaps in chain mail and drive past the gambeson to cause damage. Others were forged with wide barbs, and the width of the barbs made withdrawing the arrow a difficult and painful process. Even if the width of the barbs resulted in a slower entry into the victim and thus a shallower wound, an enemy slipping into shock and howling in pain as he tries to pull a barbed arrow out of his body is no more dangerous than a dead man.

Archers and other English infantry had two competing factors in choice of armour. One was protection against attack, and the other was ability to run away. Archers had little defence in close combat except perhaps for a knife or club, or perhaps a sword for a wealthy peasant or tradesman. As such, when presented with an enemy at short range their best recourse was to run rather than try to fight. So there was little point in lugging armour with them, and little point in buying them armour. Indeed, in King Edward I's issue of the Assizes, the people who are expected to bring bows are not expected to bring armour. Those men who were summoned to carry polearms (poles from six to ten feet with a heavy blade attached) were also not required to have armour, but if they expected to survive an encounter with another man similarly armed they would have perhaps an iron hat, a padded gambeson, and perhaps even a chain mail shirt handed down from the booty of some long-forgotten battle.

Their clothing was simply cut: a shirt, stockings, and a few layers of thick coats. Their clothes were looser cut than those of the knights, and the sleeves did not have the exaggerated hanging tippets. A mantlel and a separate hood offered protection from the elements as well as the closest thing to a bed the soldiers could expect. The clothes would be made of wool and leather and some linen or even expensive cotton. Clothes were decorated with jewellery, buttons and embroidery, as well as the decoration of brightly-dyed cloth for the men who could afford it.

It is possible to guess at the staple food offered to the soldiers by the orders from the royal treasury. Wheat and oats for bread were ordered in huge quantities along with beans and pease for bread and porridge. Dried fish was ordered in similar quantities. Smaller quantities were ordered of bacon and wine, possibly to be reserved for the consumption of those used to better food.

The Harrow

Edward I's generals, many of whom were also Edward II's generals, were not quite so fixated upon the glorious charge with fixed lance as one is tempted to believe. It is easy to judge Bannockburn by saying that King Edward expected to fight a cavalry battle, that he tried to, and that he failed. However, this judgement is unfair. The English generals (and I use the term loosely; they did not wear red tabs on their tunics) had several years' experience fighting wars with the Scots and the Welsh. Those years were not spent fighting chivalric battles of charges and ransoms, but bloody actions in which English archers, billmen and horsemen combined to massacre Welsh knifemen and Scottish spearmen. This was, as might be expected, difficult to reconcile with the chivalric ethic. The Falkirk Roll, a roll of arms which celebrates the victory at Falkirk, describes the coat of arms of each knight banneret at the battle, battalion by battalion, completely ignoring the fact that it was the humble archer who broke the Wallace's schiltrons so that the English horse could ride down the humble Scots soldiers.

Armed with this experience, the English sought to deploy their troops so that they could work in concert with each other. The language of the time refers to archers deployed in a formation called a herce. A herce is a rake used in place of a harrow, which is a farming implement consisting of a grid spiked on the bottom, which is dragged across a field by some draught animal. The term herce also refers to a sort of church chandelier which was a triangular grid with spikes pointing upwards (to hold candles) rather than downwards. Modern English recalls the use of the herce to carry corpses from church to churchyard in the word 'hearse'. The term might refer to a triangle, modelled on the church herce, or to a gridded layout of troops, or indeed to a combination of a triangular formation of archers set in a grid. A wedge pointing towards the enemy would, after all, present the archers from two sides of the formation towards the enemy, while a rectangle allows only the archers of one side a direct field of fire.

In any event, the herces of troops were laid out in alternation of archers and foot soldiers and horse. A rough description of the deployment of English troops in the Welsh wars is that horse alternated with archers in the front line. Sometimes this was achieved by alternating bodies of knights and foot soldiers, and sometimes by alternating one horse and one archer. It seems to have been important to the knights that they dominate the front line, as a mounted centre, and this has the advantage of allowing them an aggressive role should they seek to attack. More importantly, the knights provide protection for the archers. If the enemy horse tried to charge the archers as the English horse did successfully against the Scottish archers at Falkirk, then the horsemen beside the archers can themselves charge, thus forcing the opposing knights to stop to fight instead of attacking the archers.

Only after Bannockburn were English knights routinely dismounted to fight battles entirely on foot, and at Halidon Hill (in 1333) King Edward III dismounted all of his knights (including himself), and fought on foot with his archers shooting from the flanks. Thus the dismounted knights could defend the archers from cavalry attack, while the archers shot at the pikemen. This proved to be effective against the Scottish foot soldiers, and that later Plantagenet set the Scots to flight without the English sustaining serious losses.

The cavalry in their battalions were packed tightly together, the knights riding shoulder-to-shoulder and spur-to-spur. They faced the enemy in bunches, one or two knights deep, with the lesser horsemen behind to take advantage of the disorder when the lines degenerated into the chaos of attack. There was no need for a complicated set of commands: the only tactic the knights knew was the charge, and the only commands were to bring the horses up to speed preparatory to attacking. There was no need for a chain of command, since the only decision that remained once the knights were on the field was when to begin the charge. Each battalion knew its commander by his banner and his shield, and after the first charge they were expected to rally to the leader, but once the constables had pushed and prodded the knights into their lines at the beginning of the battle the leader had little to offer his men but a hearty shout of his battle-cry. After the initial charge, each leader might decide to re-form and charge again, or he might decide to mix in with the enemy at sword's point.

When Edward II deployed his troops for battle on Stirling carse, he set up a line of units abreast. On his left and right flanks were his archers; in the centre was his horse. This is the textbook deployment of an Edwardian English army, the deployment that won Wales, that was successful in Scotland and that was so effective again and again against the French in the Hundred Years' War. If their way was blocked by Scottish pikemen, the archers could advance while shooting, and stop within bowshot but outside of spear range. The Scottish horse could be headed off by the English knights, and it would be Falkirk all over again. In the more likely event that Scottish armies harried them without openly attacking, the horde of foot soldiers could be sent after them, to chase them through woods and wrestle them in swamps.

The army, diverse as it was, had to be brought to one place to be set against the Scots. The appointed place was Wark, on the English side of the River Tweed opposite Berwick.

The Muster – Wark-on-Tweed

The first part of the English army began to gather in the spring of 1314, at Newcastle-upon-Tyne, with the earls who would be the leading men of the expedition. The chairman of this committee of earls was Aylmer de Valence, the Earl of Pembroke, recently appointed guardian of Scotland and king's lieutenant. Pembroke, forty-four years of age, was a powerful man with estates spread over France. He is known to history as an honourable and a chivalrous man, but he was always willing to respond to realpolitik rather than to the codes of knighthood. When the newly-crowned King Robert offered single combat to decide who would hold the city of Perth, Pembroke agreed. Then, in the middle of the night before the scheduled duel, Pembroke's men fell upon the sleeping Scots and massacred them. Years before, when Piers Gaveston offered to surrender himself from Scarborough Castle in return for his own life, Pembroke agreed. Then, one night while Pembroke was conveniently away visiting his wife, the Earl of Lancaster came and took Gaveston away to be murdered. When all is said and done, though, Pembroke seems to have had a genuine interest in the proper governance of England and the subjugation of Scotland.

The king's brother-in-law, Humphrey de Bohun, the Earl of Hereford and Essex, came to the muster. Though he had sided with the king's enemies over the matter of Piers Gaveston and had to be included in the general pardon of 1313, he had special reason to come to Scotland. On the coronation of King Robert in 1306, Edward Longshanks had deeded the Bruce lands of Annandale to Hereford; therefore, if the Bruce were defeated, vast estates would be added to Hereford's possessions. Perhaps King Edward mentioned to him that if he did not come along on this expedition, and if this expedition was successful, then Annandale might be given to a more helpful nobleman. Almost since the first Bohun was made Earl of Hereford in 1141, they had passed from father to son the office of constable of England, but such a high office did not necessarily encourage participation. For example, Lancaster himself, the king's arch-enemy, was steward of England, and he found something better to do in the spring of 1314. With Hereford, thirty-eight years of age, came his nephew Henry de Bohun, a young knight out to make a name for himself.

Another royal brother-in-law who came was Gilbert de Clare, the Earl of Gloucester and Hertford. He was just twenty-three years old, and only two years before, his son John had died in infancy. Gloucester was distinguished not only by being Captain in Scotland and the North – ranking him just after Pembroke in the army's pecking order – but by being related to an astonishing number of the participants in this adventure. By dint of assiduous arranging of marriages on the part of his father and grandfather, he was related to King Robert by blood as well as to King Edward, Hereford and the unfortunate Piers Gaveston by marriage. Unlike Pembroke, who had ventured from one side of the Gaveston controversy to the other, and unlike Hereford, who had stayed on the side of the earls, Gloucester had remained on the side of the king until it seemed that the king must be overthrown or the kingdom might disintegrate into chaos.

A Scottish earl, the Earl of Angus, responded to the summons. With him were a number of Scottish knights who had decided that their allegiance to their English sovereign was more important than their allegiance to the claimant to the Scottish throne. Some, like John Comyn, had ample reason to prefer Plantagenet rule to Bruce. The Earl of Atholl, another Scot, nursed a grudge against the Bruce, and while he would not come to Wark, he would make his own contribution to the English war effort by destroying the Scottish supply centre at Cambuskenneth Abbey the night before the Battle of Bannockburn.

It is impossible to determine with certainty the number of people who arrived at Wark-on-Tweed, across the river from Berwick, between 10-17 June 1314. A good guess is that there were about 15,000 foot soldiers and 2,500 cavalry, rather a large army for medieval England. With them there were thousands of men and women who provided ancillary services to the army. There had to be farriers and grooms to tend to the horses, both the warhorses and the transport horses. There were cooks, barbers, cobblers, carpenters, sappers and other tradesmen. There were minstrels, heralds, valets, laundresses, prostitutes and other servants of all sorts. Priests in their hundreds were there to confess the living and shrive the dying. Every cart and every wagon had its driver, and many carts and wagons carried nothing but fodder. To provide this secondary army King Edward ordered his sheriffs to round up 'all ecclesiastical persons and women and other persons unable to labour... who ought to do the king service' and bring them in the middle of June to Berwick. Fines were specified for those who did not respond, and those fines would likely be used to pay the expenses of those who came. The skilled workers were engaged separately: Master John of Came hiring one hundred masons for the rebuilding of the English fortresses, Roger de Chalk hiring one hundred carpenters, and Edward Smith hiring thirty smiths.

Earls and rich knights had large establishments with tents, staffs of servants and wagons of goods. The king expected to set up a summer base at Stirling, so an abridged version of the royal household was packed in wagons and brought along, with clerks and supplies of paper and ink and wax. The Great Seal was brought, and documents flowed uninterrupted from the travelling court all along the king's route. At Berwick the chancery stopped, and under the care of the Archbishop of Canterbury continued the routine business of the court throughout the campaign.

All the noblemen, including the sheriffs and the earls, brought their foot soldiers with them to Wark. Between there and Stirling the knights ceased to concern themselves with their own foot soldiers, leaving them to the supervision of constables. The cavalry joined battalions composed of other knights and their 'lances'. It is possible that several lances were commanded by a knight banneret, distinguished by the square banner on his lance. However, the title of banneret indicated a knight's rank and qualification rather than his position in the chain of command. The cavalry was divided into ten battalions, each composed of roughly eighty lances and each supervised by a paramount banneret.

The ordering of the army on the march was the responsibility of the constables. The office originates with the 'comes stabuli' of the Frankish kings – the ruler of the stables. Since cavalry combat was the sort of warfare practiced by the governing élite, the chief of the stables came to be an important fellow, in charge of the entire army. The chief of all the constables was the constable of England, the Earl of Hereford. At Wark, King Edward appointed an additional chief of the constables, the Earl of Gloucester. Jointly they commanded the first battalion.

The king's marshalcy was a subsidiary function of the constable's office. The marshals were concerned with feeding, littering, shoeing, doctoring and other requisites of the horses. When not on campaign the marshalcy was also concerned with breeding horseflesh. The office of the marshal of England grew in importance; eventually only earls held the job, and they were called Earls Marshal. After the execution of the last hereditary constable of England in the sixteenth century, the Earl Marshal became the most important military officer in the royal household.

The infantry were shepherded by the constables who inspected their arms twice a year. There were two constables for each hundred (a hundred is a measure of land, like a township, not one hundred men), with duties similar to those of the marshal in the Wild West: representing the central government (such as it was) as a combination of policeman and prosecuting attorney. The organisation of infantry for the field was a matter of folk custom, and not recorded by knights nor by the minstrels and chroniclers they employed, but in theory at least they were divided into groups of ten and one hundred, like their Roman predecessors.

They may in practice have been grouped in sections of twenty, which were combined to form a larger unit known as a 'conroy'. For these part-time soldiers, however, bonds of family and community were far more important than notions of military order.

The town of Berwick had been prepared to act as the base of operations for this campaign. Years before, the people of Berwick had been encouraged to rebuild the walls that the Scots had destroyed, and in late 1313 they were offered extra funds from the customs at their own port as a prize if they finished quickly. Berwick, on the south bank of the river Tweed, was the southernmost link in the chain of English fortresses in Scotland (though Berwick is today in England), and King Edward expected to rebuild the chain.

The summons that went out to the men and women of England commanded them to come to Wark-on-Tweed (the suburb across the river from Berwick) on Monday 10 June. The army was fully mustered, taken across the river and ready to depart by the next Monday (17 June), leaving a week's time to march to Stirling. It is about 80 kilometres (50 miles) through Lauderdale from Berwick to Edinburgh. It is another 32 kilometres (20 miles) from Edinburgh to Falkirk and another 32 kilometres (20 miles) to Stirling. The summer days were long, giving plenty of time for breaking camp, marching and making camp at the end of the day. Water was plentiful, and supplies waited for them at Edinburgh, their halfway mark.

The first leg of 80 kilometres was done in a leisurely four days. They marched along Dere Street, the old Roman Road, through the beautiful summertime countryside beneath the hills of Lammermuir. By the time they had got to Edinburgh, Friday 21 June, only three days remained before the garrison at Stirling would surrender to the Scots. The remaining 70 kilometres had to be marched in two days. Marching 20 miles in a day did not require marching quickly, just marching long hours, with fewer stops to rest. It was not difficult for the folk of the army to fall asleep in the long, bright evening of 22 June when they reached Falkirk.

5

The Scottish Army

The Tor Wood

As soon as King Robert heard the grim news of the Earl of Carrick's bargain with Mowbray, he knew that within a year an English army would march north to relieve Stirling. It did not take long for the further news to reach King Robert: that the English army would muster in June at Wark-on-Tweed. Their course from Wark would have to be from there to the English stronghold at Edinburgh, where the great flotilla of English ships would provision the army.

King Robert needed to muster his army somewhere between Wark and Stirling. The Lothian fortresses were firmly in English hands, making it difficult indeed for King Robert to muster his army in Lauderdale, between Wark and Edinburgh. Should the Scots have done poorly in Lauderdale, it would have been a long, harried march for a defeated army back across the Forth to safety. Robert the Bruce was not willing to risk everything on this campaign, and so he chose a site closer to Stirling, where there was the possibility of easy refuge in the nearby hills to the west and the north.

Between Falkirk and Stirling lies the Tor Wood, an ancient hilly forest. Here the Scottish army could be assembled and trained, living off the land thereabouts. King Robert's troops were summoned to come to the Tor Wood at the end of April. They had about a month to train, from the day of muster to the expected date of the English army's arrival.

Money

The king of Scots ruled a poor country. Unlike the king of England, who ruled a potentially rich source of funds for war, the king of Scots needed to scrounge every penny for an expedition. The Lowlands of Scotland were not fertile enough to support more than a few hundred knights, and without the additional support of English estates, knights were thin on the ground. Unlike King Edward, King Robert could not afford to bring foreign knights to Britain for the campaign.

Even a low-budget war is expensive. Revenues of his lands would help, but soldiers are hungry men and need to be fed. The chiefs of the highland tribes would need to be bribed. Iron needed to be bought for horseshoes, for spear-points and for helmets. Even an army composed mostly of tribesmen and common husbandmen needed its supporting force of wagons and teamsters, blacksmiths, barbers, carpenters and sappers.

To exact stiff taxes on his noblemen and freemen would have been to send them over to the English camp. Already the nobles must have felt the bite of being separated from the wealth of the English lands and court: to tax them would be to alienate them.

Lothian, the southernmost province of Scotland, was some of the best farmland in the kingdom. Whatever the political leanings of the individual farmer, control of the land was vested in the Earl of Dunbar, an English client. It was his responsibility to protect Lothian on behalf of the Plantagenet, and to punish those who acted against his English overlord. To reap revenues in Lothian would be to attack the Earl of Dunbar and through him the king of England. The common folk of Lothian would direct their fury against the Bruce only in an indirect sense. The close target of their anger would be Dunbar, whose brief was to protect them.

A few miles across the imaginary line that separated England and Scotland there was more money to be had. The cities of Carlisle, Berwick and Durham were there, as well as smaller towns. The north was home to monasteries which had been the recipients of noblemen's donations for centuries. Herds of cattle were kept in the English countryside, fat and mobile. King Robert ran no risk of alienating the English of the north, for they were already his enemies. Far from any common Celtic bond of resistance to London, to the northerners the Scots were predators to be feared.

Between 1310 and 1314, Scottish expeditions ravaged Lothian and the north of England. Where they could get cattle, they rustled it, driving it across the border and into Scotland. In cities and monasteries they levied the blackmail, pointing out to the mayor or to the abbot that it was a very nice place he had, and it would be a pity if something happened to it. A mayor or abbot had a choice: resist loyally and count on the king of England to revenge the smouldering ruin of your town, or pay the protection money and explain to King Edward that you had no choice but to betray him. In the event, the presence of a Scottish army generally tipped

the scales in favour of paying the Scots, and protesting fever-
ishly to London.

Turnout

We can only guess at the English turnout for the campaign
to relieve Stirling Castle. Just so it is difficult to determine
which of the nobles of Scotland came to the Bruce's camp in
the Tor Wood in the Spring of 1314. The nature of King
Robert's army makes its composition especially difficult to
determine. It consisted of knights whose lots were tied to
Bruce's, and those whose fortunes would fail if a Plantagenet
or his puppet Comyn returned to the guardianship of
Scotland. They brought with them the men from their estates
who had been fighting guerrilla actions against the English
every summer for more than twenty years. Along came the
Islemen and Highland chiefs with their fighting tails, arriving
for friendship with the Bruce, for the bribes he paid with
money from Carlisle and Durham, and for the booty that
would follow a victory. Those who thought that King Robert
would lose and who were able to, stayed away. This last
accounted for a large number, and there cannot have been
more than 5,000 foot soldiers mustered in the Tor Wood.

There were four great Scots lords who came with their
men. One was Edward Bruce the Earl of Carrick, who
brought with him men from the Bruce wardship of Mar,
from the conquered Comyn lands of Buchan, from Galloway
and from Aberdeenshire. Another was Thomas Randolph the
Earl of Moray, who brought men from Moray, Ross and
Nithsdale; all inflamed to war by the years of preaching from
the bishop of Moray. Young Walter the Steward came with his

men from Renfrew and Lanarkshire, all to be commanded by the Black Douglas who brought his Bordermen as well. Robert Keith the great marshal of Scotland brought with him a small force of light horsemen. King Robert himself brought his own men from Carrick, as well as men from the western Highlands and the Isles, warlike men who could afford to leave their flocks at pasture for the summer. When King Edward sent to Richard de Burgh, the Earl of Ulster, commanding him to bring men to muster at Wark, Ulster did not come, and he might well have sent his men to fight on the side of his son-in-law King Robert.

The Templars

The Order of the Poor Knights of the Temple was in 1307 no longer poor, nor did it fulfil its old mission of protecting travellers to and from the Holy Sepulchre from its barracks at the Temple Mount in Jerusalem. After the end of the Latin kingdom of Jerusalem in 1291 the order resembled nothing so much as a multinational corporation. Although the Templars were, first and foremost, an army of fighting priests, their functions after 1291 had more to do with banking and politics than with holy war.

The Templars were responsible only to the Pope. Some kings did not mind this, and richly endowed the Templars in their kingdoms. King Philip le Beau of France, however, was not of such a mind. His kingdom had within it a large number of Templar commanderies, and the Temple in Paris controlled French royal finances. Where it had once been useful to crusading French kings to have ready credit at the Templar commanderies in the Holy Land, now their royal treasury was in the hands of an independent army. So long as the Pope was an independent Roman prince, and the Templars responsible only to the Pope, this state of affairs could continue. Once the papacy became a French subsidiary, however, the Temple was no longer so secure on its foundations.

The Order of the Temple was accused of various horrible crimes, including but not limited to sacrilege, sodomy, buggery and blasphemy. The Templars saw which way the wind was blowing, and (except for a few knights) they repented their sins, spent a few years in jail and were pardoned in 1312. By executive order of the Pope, the Templars were dissolved, and their property given over to their rival order the Hospitallers. The king of France kindly took custody of the Templars' property, and deducted a service charge before passing the goods along to their new custodians.

The individual Templars faded into other orders, and there is no further documentary evidence on the subject after 1312. There is an interesting Masonic legend which has it that the order continued in Scotland and became the Scottish rite of freemansonry. This legend claims that since the memorandum suppressing the knights was never promulgated in Scotland, the order continued there in secret. Templar knights, therefore, participated at Bannockburn, and in even later battles. It is easy to dismiss this legend as romantic rubbish. I do. It is, however, quite possible that former Templars served on both sides of the field at Bannockburn.

Knights

The Scottish knights were not very different from English knights, or indeed knights throughout western Christendom.

They shared the same values, swore the same oaths and held them in the same regard as their English counterparts. There were Scottish knights on the English side of the field at Bannockburn, whether because they were dispossessed of their Scottish lands, like Ingraham de Umfraville, or because of implacable opposition to the Bruce, like John and Edmund Comyn, who were out to avenge their murdered kinsman, the Red Comyn. They all spoke versions of the Anglo-Norman dialect of French, listened to the same chivalric epics sung by troubadours and played the same games. Bonds of consanguinity and affinity crossed the field at Bannockburn at all levels. The king of Scots himself was descended from the same grandfather as the Earl of Gloucester, who faced him across the field.

One fact which governed the Scottish knights was the availability of horses. Destriers were scarce enough in England to command a high price when imported from Spain and France. An immense allocation of English resources went to breeding and maintaining the stock of big warhorses. Scotland, so much poorer and more remote, was even harder to supply with good warhorses. Whether it was this matter of horse-economics, or more clever considerations of tactics, the mounted knights who rode with Keith the Marshal were not mounted like their English foes. They sat small horses, which could carry the same weight as a destrier but could not run as fast. The reduction in speed meant that they did not ride with couched lances, or in huge saddles. These soldiers were called 'hobelars', after the 'hobby-horses' that they rode. They either relied on their swords, or carried light lances like the ones used by their Norman for-bears at Hastings. Against a fully-armoured knight their weight would be insufficient to unseat the sheer mass of their opponents. Against foot soldiers, however, they sacrificed only some of the *Schrecklichkeit* of the mounted charge in return for infinitely superior manoeuvrability. The English used hobelars in Wales, and might also have brought some along on their Stirling campaign.

Spearmen

A spear is not a difficult weapon to produce. The shaft can be made of the trunk of a sapling, producing a resilient piece of wood as long as eighteen feet that is reasonably straight and that is difficult to break. The head is a knife-blade, the sort that any reasonably skilled blacksmith can produce. It does not need to meet the finicky requirements of a sword, and it does not need the specialised craftsmanship that a sword requires. This makes the spear a cheap and available weapon.

An English or French peasant called up to war had some ready-made weapons. Given a bit of fiendish creativity, any farm implement can be used to hurt someone. English armies had no shortage of men with scythes, sickles, bills and other sorts of pruning-hooks that could be easily mounted on a six- to ten-foot pole and be used to menace the enemy. There were undoubtedly some Scottish soldiers who could provide farming implements for use as weapons, but there were many who were herdsmen, and they did not have the same panoply of dangerous equipment to bring with them to war.

The brown bill that was the staple of the English peasant fighter (before they all turned into archers in 1337 just in time for the Hundred Years' War) had severe limitations. When used against an archer, the heavy bladed tools might be effective, but how to get within six or so feet of an archer without having a yard-long dowel put through the bowel? When used against another side equipped with the same weapons, the tendency is for each side to stay out of the other side's range. The result is a stand-off, with victory going to the side with enough men to withstand attrition, to the side with enough courage or stupidity to seize the initiative and attack the other side and frighten them into disorder, or to the side which out-manoeuvres the other. All those options make it the responsibility of another sort of soldier – archers or knights – to swing the balance one way or the other. Against horse it is difficult to rely on a ten-foot polearm. A knight's lance could be fourteen feet long, extending it nine or so feet beyond the horse's face. A ten-foot bill held in a two-handed grip extends it only six or seven feet beyond the foot soldier. A commander can tell his men that the horses will not charge a standing line of men, but those extra four feet of lance speak strongly to Jack Billman, asking him whether the horse will indeed stop so far short of the line that Jack's body is not transfixed by the lance. The result is a game of chicken between a horse, carrying the fearsome superstructure of a knight in armour, and on the other side a man conditioned all his life to fear and respect knights as innately superior beings.

The sight of the knight was made more fearsome by certain chivalric characteristics. First, the antagonist did not look like a man. The colour of armour was black, the colour wrought iron turns when worked at the forge, familiar to us from black wrought-iron fences. This carbon deposit protects the metal from rust, and can be renewed by baking the armour in powdered charcoal. Polishing plate armour (which is a difficult and time-consuming process in the absence of modern buffing equipment) makes it a shiny dove-grey. Polishing mail (tradi-tionally by rolling it in a barrel of sand) makes it a shimmer-ing combination of black and grey. None of these colours, nor the bright colours that knights painted on their armour and shields, were the colours of human beings. The metal armour and painted cloth trappers on the horses changed them from the same sort of beast that pulled the plough into weird shape-less creatures. These towering figures, in their strange and wonderful colours, had no faces as they charged. Even those who did not wear great helms or bascinets with face-plates covered their faces with their shields. As well, the mounted knight was noisy, with jingling harness and thundering hooves that, en masse, made the ground tremble. This is not to say that the medieval peasant was so superstitious as to imagine that the knight on horseback was some supernatural being. Knights were plentiful enough that every soldier would have seen a knight shaving in the morning after a late night of drinking wine and eating baked lampreys (a sight guaranteed to convince anyone of the knight's humanity). Rather, these frightening factors, which the Germans call *Schrecklichkeit*, cre-ated a fear in the peasant or townsman that tipped the scales in this great game of chicken. With this roaring apparition before him, the billman was likely to break and run.

Once the foot soldiers began to run, the battle was over for them. Whether the knights chose to ride in among them with their maces and falchions and swords, dishing in heads and causing nasty wounds, whether the opposing foot sol-diers rushed in with their own bills to hack them apart from behind, or whether they turned to fight another foe, the foot soldiers were 'broken'; that is, they were no longer an influ-ential part of the battle.

The use of a pike or long spear changes the equation somewhat. A fourteen- to eighteen-foot spear can extend fifteen feet ahead of the man holding it. The effect of fifty men in two rows holding pikes is a wall of steel points rather than the brown bill's irregular row of men with farming implements. These extra few feet can make the difference between the soldier standing his ground and the soldier running. Here in this wall of pikes it might be possible to convince the foot soldier to keep his place. It would take a great deal of training, with knights rushing the spearmen under mock battle conditions, and perhaps a tradition of fighting with pikes against horse, to keep the men from breaking, but the Scots had both time to train and experience against horse.

The Scottish soldier's precise equipment for the Stirling campaign of 1314 is impossible to determine. Like their English counterparts they wore what armour they thought useful or could get, including at least a steel or leather cap and a padded gambeson, like the padded jack the knight wore under his armour. His hands on the pike might be covered in mail mittens. He might wear body armour of bits of iron laced together to form 'lamellar', of hardened leather or of cast-off pieces of chain and plate. It is likely that some sort of shield was strapped to the forearm, possibly similar to the later Scottish bullhide targe. Many of the men had axes, similar to spears in cheapness. Any blacksmith worth his salt could make an axe-head, and anyone with a piece of wood could make the haft. In addition, axes were everyday items which a soldier could take from his hut when called to war.

The spear was held across the body, with the left hand nearer the point, and the left shoulder pointing in the direction the spearman wished to fight. The front rank, or indeed both ranks, could kneel, putting the butt of the pike against the ground, bracing it with the right foot and aiming the point with the other two hands. This stance was excellent for receiving cavalry, not so much for bearing the shock of the charge – horses, unlike the stupid wild boar, do not keep charging once they see or feel the points of spears – but for making the men feel ready and steady.

The aggressive use of the pike as a weapon, rather than as a defence, would come after the enemy horse had closed and stopped. The disordered horsemen then became prey to the pike-points. A row of pikemen with pikes braced against the ground is a defensive thing. A pikeman who puts the steel tip of his spear against the breast of a foundering horse ten feet away, then leans into a thrust with all his weight, is an offensive weapon indeed.

The pike is useful only in a large group, tightly packed and somewhat disciplined. One-on-one, or in similar small numbers, the pike becomes unwieldy in the extreme, a dagger with a long, clumsy handle. The pikeman who wished to fight without benefit of a wall of comrades would resort to his axe, or knife, or sword.

When pikemen on foot come to fight against other infantry, the situation is dependent on many variables, just as it is with any other matched group. Then luck, nerve, skill and numbers are the deciding factors, rather than the properties of the weapons. Against archers, pikes still have the formidable obstacle of crossing ground in the face of a hail of arrows, allowing the pikemen to be killed for long minutes before their remnants can come close enough to menace the archers.

Training the Men

Most modern armies teach their soldiers the techniques of drill, that is, precisely organised marching up and down a square. These techniques are no longer directly applicable to the trade of the soldier, although they once were. Modern battles are not fought in opposing lines of armed men, but rather in very open arrangements of men and equipment. The English and Scottish armies that fought at Bannockburn were similar to modern troops in that they were not accustomed to fighting in strict formations.

The basic unit of mayhem is a mob. As police crowd-control experts know, a mob is a very unpredictable thing. A howling mob of men set on beating the daylights out of another howling mob of men is not a reliable base on which to base one's dynastic ambitions. Mob warfare is very dependent on individual skill, and on group morale. A mob might be stopped in its tracks by the sight of one of their number screaming with an arrow through his throat, or it might be spurred on by the sight. When a mob mixes in with its foes, the resulting individual combats are resolved on an individual basis, leaving someone who fancies himself a leader unable to influence the outcome.

The main endeavour of military science is increasing the influence of the commander over the mob, and thus over the outcome of the battle. The drill of today's armies is a vestige of early modern methods of military discipline and control. It is retained in modern armies because the rote learning of precise drill reinforces the habit of unthinking obedience in soldiers. This unthinking obedience is an effort to overcome both mob instincts and man's natural desire not to be killed.

The medieval commander had different ways of controlling the mob, depending on the sort of soldier. Knights were expected to bring all the passion and gusto of the mob to battle. Their ideal was to be a group of such proficient individuals, so ready with initiative and so high in morale, that they offered the best of the mob without the worst.

The common foot soldier, however, was a more difficult problem. Some soldiers were professionals, and they could afford to spend their time training and participating in military action, so that when they came to battle their commanders would know how to deal with them, and they would know how to obey their commanders. Professional soldiering was, however, a poor career in fourteenth-century Britain, where there was not a great deal of cash money being offered for military service. An Englishman or Scot with a taste for the military life was better advised to travel to the Continent where there was always opportunity for risking one's life at the wealthy behest of some Italian prince.

The common 'grunt' of wars in Britain was not a full-time soldier. He was likely a farmer or herdsman, with better things to do than learn to mark time and wheel into column. He had, by way of weapons, his farming implements or the axe he used to fell his firewood. He might know how to use a bow for taking birds and small animals. The nobleman who was required to provide a feudal levy, or the clan chieftain who was providing similar service, had the problem of providing effective troops from this base.

Scotland and Wales had certain advantages in providing foot soldiers. Both these lands are remarkable, compared with medieval England or France, for their poverty. Arable land was found in only limited parts of Scotland and Wales. The people who lived in these inhospitable places did not have crops to tend, not in the same way that a Kentish farmer did, and so the entire adult male population of a Scottish district or clan could be called up for battle. Scottish cattle could fend for themselves watched by children, where a large barley farm could not. As well, the fierce competition for resources in these countries made fighting one's neighbours a more frequent activity. Scottish and Welsh soldiers reflected this. They knew their limited range of weapons well, and they could be taken away from their lands for longer stretches of time than their English counterparts.

Robert the Bruce had fought a long campaign of hit-and-run, refusing to allow himself to be caught in the open to fight on English terms. Now, by the terms of his brother's rash oath, he was bound to meet an English army at a set time, somewhere near a set place. How, then, to turn a rabble of Scottish cowboys, shepherds, farmers and thugs into an army that could face English horse and English archery?

The Bruce had an example to follow. In 1302 an army of Flemish commoners had faced an army of French knights across a field at Courtrai. The Flemings watched as the French charged towards them, fearsome on their great warhorses. The foot soldiers were armed with spears and the knowledge that there was a canal between them and the French. When the French horses were stopped by the canal, the Flemings advanced and attacked the knights, killing many and causing the rest to flee for their lives.

The idea of solving the howling-mob problem by forming foot soldiers into formations was by no means a new one. The Romans inherited it from the Greeks' phalanx, and passed it on. The English foot soldiers at Hastings formed a wall of shields against the Norman horse. These are only a few examples of a very effective use of a simple piece of hardware: the shield.

The Problem of Formation

A man can only face in one direction at a time. He can only fight someone he is facing, with his effectiveness diminishing the closer his enemy is to facing his back. Thus it is in the interest of an attacker to attack his enemy from the side or back. The first defence against this is forming the soldiers into a line. With, say, ten men in a line there are only two men whose sides are exposed to the enemy. If the enemy attacks from the rear, everyone need only turn around, and once again there are only two sides exposed. So long as the men all stand shoulder-to-shoulder, and thus have only two flanks for the lot of them, their likelihood of being caught on a flank is reduced.

On the other side of the field is a group which is now encouraged to attack on one of those two flanks. An attack on an enemy's flank forces the man on the flank to turn to defend himself. Once he has turned, he is no longer shoulder-to-shoulder with his comrades, and the next man down the line is more vulnerable. If the line keeps its formation, the attacking soldiers can kill them one by one. If the defenders rush to defend their friends, they can be killed before they can form a new line. A great deal of the theory of infantry warfare is protection of flanks from this sort of crisis.

The various evolutions, such as wheels and oblique marching, taught to modern soldiers can help a group of soldiers to escape being flanked. If the line moves out of the way or turns to meet the attacking line face-to-face, the flank is safe. A line need not be straight to reap the benefits of standing shoulder-to-shoulder. It can be wedge-shaped, with the flanks raked back, away from the enemy, or cup-shaped with the flanks raked forwards. Different expedients can be taken to protect a flank against attack, with varying levels of difficulty and training.

All these expedients for protecting a flank become more difficult when the equation is complicated by different sorts of forces. A straight line will not avail against good archers, indeed a straight line of standing men makes the archer's job easier. Cavalry is also a problem: a troop of horsemen can move very quickly and change direction much faster than men can move in formation. Even a group trained to execute manoeuvres on the drill square might have a great deal of trouble doing so while they are being picked off by archers, or hit from the flank or the rear by cavalry.

The infantry square that began to be developed in the later Middle Ages by the Swiss, and which reached its apotheosis at Waterloo, is an effective formation for combating these problems. An infantry square consists, essentially, of four lines of men joined at right angles. Thus the infantry square bristles with pikes or bayonets at every hand, with no vulnerable flank. Reinforcements stand within the square, and can be pushed into place by sergeants in order to fill the places of dead or injured men. However, keeping the precise lines and angles necessary for manoeuvring a line or maintaining a square requires a great deal of training. Months of drill are necessary in order to allow a group of several hundred men to quickly form square or to wheel their lines to the right without the whole thing degenerating into chaos. Even maintaining a straight line at a slow march in one direction is difficult, and requires the constant attention of sergeants. In order to make a square useful on the field, it must be able to move as a square, or move as a series of lines that can form a square in seconds, and either is difficult indeed. These resources of training and execution were not available to the Bruce's army as it assembled in the Tor Wood. They had only a month to train, and their soldiers were hardly indoctrinated in the sort of unthinking discipline which is a prerequisite for complicated infantry evolutions. Rather than the somewhat inhuman soldiers standing in squares that Frederick the Great could move about like chess-pieces, the soldiers who came to Bannockburn were fully human, and not conditioned to march in step.

The Schiltron

The basic formation of the Scottish foot soldiers at the Battles of Falkirk, Loudon and later at Bannockburn was the schiltron. The term 'schiltron', or 'schiltrome', translated into modern English, means 'shield-wall'. The term 'wall' indicates to the modern reader a straight line, however walls need not be straight, and especially in medieval fortifications they were often round. It is quite clear, from various sources, that the schiltron was a roughly round wall of men.

Upon examination, the circular schiltron proves to be a splendid formation for foot soldiers. It is easy to maintain, even on the move, it is difficult to breach, and it allows its commanders to remain very close to the action of the battle without unnecessary risk. It is formed by taking a line, and bending it until the flanks meet. The result is in theory a circle, but the resulting wall is more likely a rough oblong. Sergeants could keep the circle from shrinking as men were killed by filling the space with men from groups of reserves within the ring.

This is not to say that the schiltron was composed of only one ring of soldiers. Concentric rings of men provide greater resilience to outside pressure. Trusted veterans, acting like modern sergeants, stand within the ring and keep up an outward pressure. So long as the outward pressure is roughly equal on all sides, the schiltron will remain roughly round. If a group of horsemen rides round the side of the schiltron, there will be no particular effect, since the men, like a great hedgehog, are protected on every side.

The fatal foible of the schiltron was demonstrated at the Battle of Falkirk. There William Wallace had his schiltrons deployed on a narrow stretch, rings of men with rope and timber laid out to keep their shape. He had cavalry ready to attack English archers. When the English horse attacked, they could find no entry into the hedgehogs without falling afoul of the spiny bristles of pikes, and the added defence of an arrow or two. In order to keep the Scottish horse from charging and dispersing the English archers, the English cavalry attacked the Scots horse, and while the Scots horse were thus occupied the English archers begin to shoot. Against the archers, those previously under-used yeomen whom Edward I was discovering use for, the schiltrons had no defence. They had few archers, if any, and they could only stand there and die. More accurately, they could realise that they were doomed, and begin making urgent travel plans for home. Once the Scots began to melt away the English horse could attack again, and this time there was no organised hedge of pikes to stop their horses. The Scots were massacred as they fled.

The only defence against attrition for a schiltron is to take the advantage of time away from the opposition. The English archers at Falkirk had all the time in the world to take their shots, limited only by their supply of arrows. It was imperative, if schiltrons were to be any use against the Plantagenet's Stirling campaign, that they be able to press an attack. They needed to minimise the period of vulnerability when the schiltrons were within bowshot of their enemies but outside of pike range, when the schiltrons could be attacked but could not themselves attack.

So the schiltron needed to be able to move. This was not difficult to do, so long as each man kept track of his neighbour, and so long as the sergeants maintained outward pressure. If the sergeants at the side facing their goal increased their pressure on the men before them, by shouting or by pushing bodily, and the sergeants in back decreased their pressure, whether by shouting or by pulling bodily, the amoeba-like formation of the schiltron would deform a bit (especially by widening at the sides), and then move as a unit. Sergeants could deal with minor deformations with a good shove here and there. If a dead horse blocked the schiltron's path, the sergeants would need to push their men to walk over it, else a dimple would form in the wall. If a few enemy soldiers tried to hack their way through the wall, the sergeants might part their men to allow the attackers to enter the amoeba, where they could be digested by the reserve soldiers within. In this way it was possible to move a schiltron quite briskly across a field without losing much of the formation's integrity.

At the risk of taking the amoeba analogy too far (the soldiers at Bannockburn certainly never imagined microorganisms), the schiltron had a nucleus. Standing in the middle were the officers. Each schiltron had a commander; let us call him a captain. The captains of each of the schiltrons were directly responsible to the king of Scots. These captains were allowed a great deal of discretion and were given a great deal of responsibility. The Earl of Moray was chided by the Bruce for not moving with alacrity against Lord Clifford's foray on the first day of the battle, making it clear that it had been Moray's responsibility as captain of a schiltron to use it when he saw an opportunity or a need. All these captains were quite close to the centre of the fray, with only a few rings of soldiers, some reserves and banner-bearers between them and their enemies.

Scottish knights, dismounted, also formed part of the nucleus. Knights or heralds were needed to identify the prisoners. It was very difficult for a mobile formation like a schiltron to hold prisoners, thus the Scots needed to be very efficient in their capture. Ordinary men-at-arms and squires held little potential for ransom, and could thus be killed within the schiltron. Scottish knights could identify wealthy enemy knights by their heraldic clothing so that they could be spared for ransom.

The amoebic analogy breaks down when it comes to archers (amoebas have no missile weapons). Scottish archers played no great part in the battle, and indeed there was no great Scottish tradition of long bow archery upon which to base a great force of powerful bows. The Earl of Moray's schiltron, with Lord Clifford's troop of horse riding near at close range, does not seem to have shot any arrows at Clifford's men or horses. Some archers from the Bruce's own lands in Ettrick were probably there, but there is no particular record of their achievements. It is quite possible that the 'archers' were told to sling their bows, then given spears and shields and put into the line with the rest of the troops. There was not likely a strong ethic of demarcation of trades among Scottish soldiers, since they were hardly a professional army. The archers might also have been put with their bows into the rings of pikes, and told to take point-blank targets of opportunity.

Looking at this medieval army, one question cries out: where are the horses? The only horsemen here are the hobelars on their hobby-horses: hardly the massed chivalry that characterise the medieval battle in the popular imagination. Some artists, desperate for horses, have depicted the captains of the schiltrons at Bannockburn sitting their horses, begging to be shot by English archers. Robert the Bruce had far fewer cavalrymen than Edward Plantagenet (what military scientists call a 'comparative disadvantage' in cavalry), and committing himself to a fight on horseback would have been foolhardy. He needed to husband his horses and commit them where they could have the most effect. In this case, he would save them for use against the fearsome English archers.

I have painted the schiltron as an ideal formation for infantry. There are, however, certain limiting factors. One is size. There is a point of limited return at which a schiltron becomes too unwieldy to move without losing its basic convex shape. As well, there is a limit to the schiltron's thickness, a point at which there are too many concentric rings, and the sergeants can no longer communicate with the troops closest to the enemy. As such, rather than muddle along with a too-large or too-thick schiltron, Robert the Bruce took the field with his army divided into four.

The Muster – Tor Wood

The army spent their month in the Tor Wood training with their pikes and axes. They knew how to use their weapons in small actions against their neighbours, but not in the seven years since the Battle of Loudon Hill was fought in 1307 had an army of Scotsmen been expected to take to the field against an English army.

The army needed to practice forming their schiltrons, getting used to running into the circle formation and being shoved by the sergeants. They needed to practice receiving cavalry, probably by kneeling in schiltron without their spears while Keith's cavalry charged, demonstrating that the horses would not run into them. This sort of training was very important indeed to the efficacy of the schiltron. It was all well and good to tell the lads that even if the Earl of Gloucester charged them, on his mucking great warhorse with his mucking great lance, the horse would not smash into them. It was altogether another thing for them to believe it. It must have taken many rehearsals, with Scottish knights charging again and again, before the infantry soldiers could sit still without flinching, let alone running away. This period of training was also useful for deciding who would be best placed in the outer rings of the schiltrons and who in the inner.

The Retreat

On 22 June, the English army marched from Edinburgh to Falkirk. The next day they would pass through the Tor Wood, and while that forest was a good place to muster the Scots, the Bruce had a better place in mind for fighting the English.

He would move his army to the New Park, towards Stirling and away from the English along the old Roman road. Bruce's manoeuvre is usually called a retreat, since it involved moving away from the enemy.

The Scots did not march from the Tor Wood to the New Park in their schiltrons, but this was not necessary. So long as each man knew where his buddies were and his sergeant could scream at them, the schiltron could be quickly formed. During the retreat from the Tor Wood to the New Park, the battalions were deployed as for the march: a vanguard at the front (the north, in the direction of Stirling), a main body of two battalions side by side, and a rear guard of his own battalion, closest to the English.

The formation of the Scots for this retreat seems designed for an ambush in the thick forest of the New Park. The Scots were prepared to be pursued by the English across the meadow between the Tor Wood and the New Park. There the rear guard would fight the English and do the best damage they could. Then the Scottish rear guard would fall back, moving northwards into the New Park to St Ninian's Kirk. The English who followed would meet a combined force of the rear guard and the vanguard. As they prepared to fight this new threat, the two schiltrons positioned to either side of the road would attack, and do what damage they could. If enough English were left to continue to attack, the Scots could cross Stirling Bridge and melt away into the hills.

This was the Bruce's plan for the Battle of Bannockburn. Like most battle plans, it had very little to do with what actually happened.

6

The Place

Stirling's important position on the narrow neck of Scotland has already been discussed. The River Forth flows down from the mountains near Ben Lomond on the west coast of Scotland and into the North Sea, on the east coast of Scotland. This describes a very steep, narrow watershed on the west side of the Lomond range of the Grampians; and the east side of the mountains is not much shallower in its pitch. Thus, there is a steep ridge on the west side of Scotland's very shallow central plain. The uppermost part of this plain, against the east side of the mountains, is the carse of Stirling.

The carse was once a combination of peat bog and cultivated fields. Its eastern and northern ends are a low-lying area called 'the Polls'. The western end is a slope that rises to meet the foothills of the Grampians, and the carse ends at the New Park, an old hunting preserve. The southern end is bounded by the Tor Wood, a wooded region of hills or 'tors'.

The peat of the carse has been harvested over the years, changing entirely the character of the site. Parts of the New Park remain, but there is no indication of the shape or extent of the old forest, save rough descriptions in property deeds. Sea level has changed over the years, altering the high tide line and thus the extent of the marsh. It is no longer possible to ascertain precisely what the character of any given bit of ground was. For the purposes of this investigation I have made a crude extrapolation from consulting old Ordnance Survey maps, and from believing others who have written on the subject, especially Professor G.W.S. Barrow.

In reading the secondary sources on the battle, we read some terms which are, to the modern reader, not clear in their meaning. One is the term 'the Polls', used to refer to part of the carse. Two erroneous identifications of the term have been advanced in the past. One is that a significant portion of the carse was mined by the Bruce with 'pots', that is to say, little pits the depth of a man's calf or a horse's cannon-bone, possibly with a spike at the bottom. These, like the pungee traps encountered in twentieth-century campaigns in southeast Asia, are designed to disable and slow advancing troops. The other erroneous identification is that the 'polls' were pools – that is, pools left behind when the tide ran out.

The Bruce mined either side of the Roman road with 'pots', at the entry to the New Park. Nonetheless, the only evidence that the carse was mined (and thus that the Bruce intended to fight on the carse) is the similarity between the words 'poll' and 'pot'. A similar homophone is invoked to identify 'polls' and 'pools'. The real story, as Barrow makes clear, is that the lower (northern and eastern) edges of the carse have since ancient times been called 'the Pows' as well as 'the Polls', and a pow is a sluggish, boggy stream. Before the peat was harvested and the water that covered the carse was diverted into a modern system of irrigation canals, the ground of the lower carse was covered with these peaty ditches.

The Site of the Battle

The First Day (Sunday)

There were (and still are) two forests near Stirling, through which the Scots army retreated followed by the English. The Tor Wood, to the south, was divided from the New Park by the Bannockburn. The New Park ran north to the great rock of Stirling, west past Gillies Hill and Coxet Hill, the beginnings of the Touch Hills and the southern range of the Grampians, and east to the bluff overlooking Stirling carse. The Roman road runs roughly north to south through both of these. On the first day of the battle, the Scottish army was in the New Park, and the English army was in the Tor Wood. The small, gentle valley between the forests, created by the flow of the burn, was where Robert the Bruce wished to fight his battle with the English. As he faced south, his right was protected by the wooded hills, his back was a forest refuge difficult for the English horse to negotiate and his left was the steep incline to the carse. He knew exactly where the English army would come, and he prepared his minefields in order to keep the English to the narrow road.

The Second Day (Monday)

To this day no one is certain of the site of the fighting on the second day of the Battle of Bannockburn. Every historian who has written about the battle has proposed his own site, based on the secondary texts, the name of the battle and the lie of the land. All of these surmises depend on dual assumptions. The first assumption is that Edward II expected to fight a pitched battle with the Scots on the morning of the 24 June. The second is that Edward Plantagenet, king of

England, was an idiot and too wilful to listen to the advice of his generals.

There are two sides to Stirling carse: the dry field and the Polls. Any site on Stirling carse is bad for fighting a cavalry battle, except the uphill dry field. The Polls were covered with mushy peat and drained by pows. A pow is the sort of muddy ditch with an overhanging bank that makes horses founder, stumble and break their legs while sinking in the mud. A carefully managed horse can be navigated around and through a field of pows, whereas several hundred horses galloping and plunging in the heat of battle are on their way to becoming part of an archaeological dig.

Two sides of the carse are bordered by the Bannockburn. On the east side of the carse lies the burn's northern run, before it spills out into the tidal bog beside the Forth. Here the burn flows within a steep ravine, until it gets to the Polls area, where it becomes shallow and mucky at low tide though it remains deep and mucky at high tide. The southern side of Stirling carse is bounded by another gully, this one through which the Bannockburn flows deep but without the tidal muck on the bottom. The eastern and south-eastern side is the most escapable, with some fording places, but still obstructed, and once past the stream, escape further eastward is blocked by more bogs. The north side is bounded by the River Forth, which we have observed is a tidal tributary of the Firth of Forth. At low tide it is deep, and where it is an easy swim to a person in a bathing suit it is impassable to a man in armour. At high tide it is marginally deeper, and the shallow banks on the south side (the carse side) are flooded, in some places for yards away from the river. Thus, any fighting position facing the Roman road is very difficult to retreat from, what with the burn always being behind. Not to say that Edwardian armies planned to retreat, but it hardly seems reasonable to deliberately fight with back against wall.

Lastly, the innate advantage of height in a battle would make the downhill side of the carse a bad place from which to launch an attack. For one thing, fighting uphill is fatiguing. For another, archers lower on a slope can see less of their targets; thus their aim is uncertain. Third: horses are harder to control when they run uphill even in peaceful situations, as they tend to speed up on an upgrade. Last: the person on the higher ground has his entire enemy as a target (except his ankles), while the person on the lower ground cannot reach his opponent's head without dangerously extending himself. This allows the uphill soldier to be more aggressive, since he need not worry so much about defending his head, whereas the downhill soldier must especially protect his head, and this restricts his visibility.

Most historians do not wonder why King Edward chose to fight with his back and left to the burn, his right to the river and the bogs and with an enemy uphill. For most historians this is not a problem. In the first place, they say, King Edward had planned to fight on marshy ground, and he brought a large number of foot soldiers for just that purpose. In the second place, they say, King Edward was a blithering idiot not disposed to heed advice, and he wanted so badly to fight a pitched battle against King Robert that he ignored all the military doctrine which had made his father's generals (who were also his generals) so successful.

Both of these excuses fall apart under a bit of argument. Although King Edward expected to fight on marshy ground and wooded hills, and therefore brought thousands of foot soldiers, he did not deploy them on 24 June, perhaps because he was not fighting in a bog at all, and perhaps because he did not expect to fight a battle that day. It must be remembered that no Scottish army had faced an Edwardian army in open, unobstructed field combat since the Bruce was forced to fight at Loudon, in May 1307, seven years before.

Nonetheless, the usual pattern of divination for historians of Bannockburn eager to place the battle is to begin with the assumption that the English set up their line to face the Scots in order to conduct a battle. Once this assumption is in train, and coupled with the fact that the English camped some-where on Stirling carse, and the Scots faced the carse from the Roman Road, the result is the conclusion that Edward II made an abysmal choice of ground for the battle. In addition, the assumption that Edward camped on the night of 23 June and deployed on the morning of 24 June with the expecta-tion of facing down a Scottish army which would come from the west makes the English king out to be incompetent in deployment as well as in choice of ground. The English army was badly deployed indeed for facing attack from the Roman road. Their forward archers were blocking their horse, their horse were blocking their rearward archers and their main body of cavalry was squeezed together in one mass. The infantry, who had been brought all the way from Wales just to fight in a swamp, were not in a position to fight at all, pos-sibly even left on the far side of the Bannockburn. A worse deployment for the English could not be conceived, unless they tried to fight across the River Forth in dinghies.

If we refrain from assuming that Edward Plantagenet was a blithering idiot, and if we also refrain from assuming that he expected to fight a pitched battle on the carse, the question of where the battle was fought changes somewhat.

35 Dere Street, the main northern road from London, runs along the eastern side of the map, past Durham and Newcastle to Edinburgh, then on to Stirling. The map makes plain why Edward chose to take this comparatively flat eastern route rather than the slightly shorter but more mountainous way through Carlisle. 'This was the road traversed by Edward I's great army of 1298 on its way to Falkirk, and this was also the road traversed by Edward II's great army on its way to Bannockburn. It will be recalled that the well-informed author of the Life of Edward II says of the army's baggage wagons that if they had been lined up together they would have stretched for twenty miles.' G.W.S. Barrow, *Land Routes: The Medieval Evidence*.

36 Glasgow is in the foreground, with Lennox immediately to the west (left) and the Bruce home country of Annandale immediately to the east (right). In the middle distance are Stirling and Edinburgh. Perth and Dundee are in the distance on the Firth of Tay. See how the massif of the Grampians in the north-west and the Firth of Forth in the east cut the Lowlands in two. 'Since we have not yet been provided with the necessary wagons for the present war in Scotland; we command you firmly enjoining that you provide and purchase at once upon reading these presents (dropping everything else) from the profits of your bailiwick for our use ten wagons and ten carts well hardwared and prepared with all their trimmings, namely each wagon having four strong horses (not pre-owned or weakened with some maiming) and each cart with eight satisfactory oxen so that the aforesaid wagons and carts thus fitted out and equipped with the aforesaid horses and oxen may be driven to Berwick upon Tweed and shall without fail be there by the 15th of John the Baptist next at the latest…'. Letter from King Edward to the Sheriff of Lincoln, from the Scottish Rolls.

37 Edinburgh and Glasgow are easy to reach from England, but an English king who wants to control Scotland has to have free access past Stirling into the lands of Strathearn and Fife beyond. Otherwise guerrillas can cross over the Forth and wreak havoc. 'In the same season of Lent [1314, the Scots] captured Edinburgh Castle in the following manner. In the evening one day the besiegers of that castle delivered an assault in force upon the [east] gate, because, owing to the position of the castle there was no other quarter where an assault could be made. Those within gathered together at the gate and offered a stout resistance; but meanwhile other Scots climbed the rocks on the north side, which was very high and fell away steeply from the foot of the wall. There they laid ladders to the wall and climbed up in such numbers that those within could not withstand them; and thus they threw open the gates, admitted their comrades, got possession of the whole castle and killed the English. They razed the said castle to the ground, just as they had done to Roxburgh Castle.' *The Lanercost Chronicle*

38 The bridge across the River Tweed was at Berwick. The English soldiers crossed there to their muster at Wark, just the other side of the bridge. Their leisurely march up the old Roman road first took them to their re-supply point at Edinburgh. 'When the king in this fashion had arranged his battles and his leadership, he rose early one morning and set out from Berwick. The English covered hills and valleys, as their broad battles rode separate over the fields. The sun was shining bright and clear, and their newly burnished armour flashed in the light, while banners blazed brightly, and pennons wved to the wind, and the whole field were aflame.' John Barbour, *The Bruce*.

39 Once past Falkirk, the English soldiers were coming close to the Scottish army. The English knew that in order to take Stirling Castle, the Scots would have to come out and fight. 'Methinks it most expedient that we go to this battle on foot, arrayed only in light armour. Our foes are in more strength and better horsed than we, and should we fight mounted we should be in great peril. But if we fight on foot, it is certain we shall always have the advantage, for in the Park among the trees the horsemen must always be encumbered, and the ditches below must also throw them into confusion.' John Barbour, *The Bruce*.

40 Actors representing knights at Bannockburn Note the round-topped helm of the knight on the right and the mail coif on the left-hand knight, who has removed his helm.

41 An actor playing an English lesser horseman rides against Robert the Bruce's schiltron. His horse is about to stop.

42 Actors representing Robert the Bruce's schiltron kneel to face the English cavalry.

43 Actors representing English knights try to turn away from Bruce's schiltron. The knight has set aside his great helm and is fighting in his bascinet.

44 Actors representing Scottish foot soldiers wear steel bascinets over mail coifs.

45 Actors representing Scottish pikemen kneel to receive the English cavalry charge.

Opposite top: 46 This view of the battlefield is from a position hovering over the Tor Wood. The English vanguard rode out to meet King Robert on the first day just below the centre of the map. The wood on the slope of Stirling rock is the modern King's Park, the remains of the vast New Park. The New Park covered the centre of the map, growing right across the Roman road (roughly the modern A872 road), where it gave way to tilled fields. The main road forded the Bannock Burn at the left-hand bridge symbol, 'the Entry'. The right-hand bridge symbol represents the ford near the site of Bannockburn village. The path from the village (now the A9 road) is shown intersecting the main road at St Ninian's Kirk. St Ninian's was about 1.6km from the entry, and Stirling about another 1.6km beyond. The high ground on the left is Gillies Hill. 'In an open field, where he thought the English must needs pass if they held their way through the Park to the castle, he caused many pits to be dug, of a foot's breadth and the depth of a man's knee. So thickly were they dug that they might be likened to the wax comb of a hive… and had covered them with sticks and green grass, that they might not easily be seen.' John Barbour, *The Bruce.*

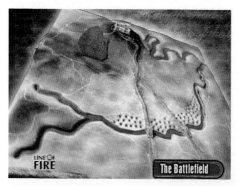

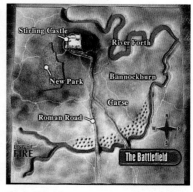

Above right: 47 The triangle of the Bannockburn, the River Forth and the wooded high ground to the west of the road is shown here. Most of the right-hand side of the map was a peat bog crossed by little streams. Clifford and Beaumont made their reconaissance in force right where the word 'Carse' appears, and stopped to fight just east of St Ninian's. Because the forests have changed shape, and even the contours of the land have changed, historians disagree about the precise location of features. This map shows the New Park much smaller than it was, though its old boundaries can only be determined roughly. It assumes that the Roman road and the Bannockburn foot-path crossed the stream over bridges, rather than fords, and it shows the 'pots' covering almost 2km of riverbank, probably too much.

Above left: 48 This view is from Skeoch, near Bannockburn village. Just past the Roman road are the small rise of Coxet Hill, and behind it the higher rise of Gillies Hill. These hills, and the road, were covered with the trees of the New Park. The English forded this stretch of the Bannock Burn, with much of the foot remaining on the south-eastern side. The English camp was just the other side of the burn, and the dry ground of Balquhidderock runs up the centre of the map towards the castle. 'The king's army... had debouched upon a plain near the water of Forth beyond Bannockburn, an evil, deep, wet marsh, where the said English army unharnessed and remained all night, having sadly lost confidence and being too much disaffected by the end of the day.' Thomas Gray of Heton, *Scalacronica*

LINE OF
FIRE

King Edward's Idiotic Plan

49 Tradition views King Edward II as a blockhead who arrayed his army with some of his archers in front, blocking his cavalry, while leaving another mob of his archers behind. Rather than being dispersed in a broad line abreast, Dean Barbour reports that the English horse were all in one mass. So when the cavalry charged, the archers to their front were forced to flee, meaning that they couldn't attack the Scottish hedgehogs of pike. The rest of the archers were too far behind the cavalry to help. This assumes stunningly poor generalship on the part of experienced soldiers like the Earl of Pembroke. It also conveniently allows the English to blame an unpopular king for a humiliating defeat. King Edward II made many sad miscalculations in his life, but this deployment was not one of them.

LINE OF
FIRE

King Edward's Real Plan

50 It is far more likely that observers were viewing a standard Edwardian army formation from one side. The archers appeared to be in front, because they were closest to the Scots army. The cavalry appeared to be all in one mass because the individual battalions were seen end-on, the gaps between them obscured. The archers were deployed on the flanks of the cavalry, or in groups alternating with the cavalry. This is strong on the offence because it allows the bowmen to shoot while the horsemen charge. The formation is also strong in the defence, allowing the archers to shoot as the enemy cavalry charges, either against the front or against the flanks. King Edward and Pembroke, his most experienced general, just didn't expect the Scottish army to appear from the woods on their left flank. When the Scots schiltrons did appear, they didn't expect them to attack, so rather than shooting at the Scots with archers, they charged the Scots with horse.

King Edward had to camp his army after the first day of the battle. He did this without knowing that it was the first day of the battle. He only knew that his vanguard and his reconnaissance party had engaged the enemy without causing serious damage. He had discovered by means of these engagements, and by means of Sir Philip Mowbray's report, that the Scots infested the New Park and blocked the Roman road. If he could find a campsite that would be defensible against surprise attack and that would allow him access to Stirling in the morning, he would be able to camp his men down for the night. After all, it was a Scottish guerrilla attack in the night that the English feared. The alternative was to spend the night on the road, sitting their horses or standing up, and this was not an option.

When on the road, King Edward was in the woods. On his left were more woods. Ahead and behind were woods. On his right was the carse of Stirling. Given that his horsemen (himself included) were vulnerable and useless in the woods, he had no choice but to camp on the carse. Given that in the morning he wanted to complete the relief of Stirling Castle, he wanted to camp on the Stirling side of the Bannockburn. Hence his campsite on the carse just north of the Bannockburn.

G.W.S. Barrow opines that the battle was fought on the Dryground of Balquhidderock, a cultivated field overlooking the most likely English campsite. This is plausible if King Edward wished merely to skirt the New Park and rejoin the Roman road around St Ninians, and if Barrow's source for the shape and location of the New Park in 1314 is correct. Militating in favour of this location is the fact that the pattern of the English advance seems to have been very much

like their column of march, leading with the vanguard, followed by the main body and then by the rear guard, as
though they met the Scots while marching westward to
regain the Roman road. However, this would require the
English to march westward up a hard grade (not a cliff, but a
climb of about 75 feet over about 300 yards, 400 if taken on
the diagonal), when their objective was in sight to the north-
west, across the reasonably flat ground along the well-
drained upper carse.

The carse was cleared of peat and mostly drained, and the
Bannockburn cut with a mill-weir, by the beginning of the
nineteenth century, changing the flows of the Pelstream and
Bannockburn, as well as the nature of the ground. We don't
know where the boggy parts of the carse were in 1314,
beyond the fact that the Polls near the tidal River Forth
were very marshy and inundated with river and seawater
twice a day. There must have been well-drained ground as
well, or the English would hardly have camped there.
Indeed, the modern pattern of streams in the upper carse
shows more than one area of high ground. There seems to
have been a broad avenue of dry ground, crossed by two relatively narrow boggy strips, that led from the English camp
to Stirling. It is quite possible that the English formed up on
a piece of dry ground in a line abreast for a march in force
across this section of the upper carse, and that the Scots
jogged down the slope from the woods, their advance
screened by Balquhidderock Wood on the brow of the hill.
It is just as possible that the English rode up the hill in the
direction of St Ninian's and were met at the top of the hill,
at Balquhidderock, by the Scots, who issued out of New
Park.

The difference between the two arguments is one of about 500 metres in distance and 75 in elevation. Even Barrow himself finds the choice between these two sites a difficult one to make, and seems to make his final decision to depict the uphill scenario at random. Pressing the balance downhill is the fact that the English seem to have had archers deployed between them and the Scots. If they were advancing up the grade at Balquhidderock in line of march, it is unlikely that a corps of archers would precede the leading horse. This narration will follow the preponderance of evidence and assume the downhill circumstances.

7

Falkirk to Bannockburn

Sunday 23 June 1314

O God of Battles! steel my soldiers' hearts;
Possess them not with fear; take from them now
The sense of reckoning, if th'opposèd numbers
Pluck their hearts from them!

King Henry V, William Shakespeare

Edward Plantagenet's army awoke in their cantonment at
Falkirk after the previous day's 32-kilometre (20-mile) march
from Edinburgh. The army's drummers woke the men while
servants broke camp and loaded the wagons. Grooms watered
the horses and oxen, hitching the teams to their carts. Barbers
shaved the rich men and trimmed their hair, then went to work
on the priests' tonsures. During the previous week's marching
they had been an army on the move. Today they would enter
the Tor Wood, where they knew the Scots were mustering, so
today they were an army preparing for battle. The knights had
been riding their palfreys, their armour packed away. Today
they rode their destriers, and they wore all their kit.

If the night's picquets started waking the sergeants at first light, it was probably dawn before the men could be got out from under their mantles. Given that the main body of the army could not move until the king and the earls were ready to go, it was at least an hour past dawn when the army was ready to march. The largest and most complicated pavilions (owned by the king and the earls) could be struck, packed and loaded onto their wagons while the main bodies of troops marched away from the campground.

Once the men were awake the army formed up in what later generations would call column of march, to distinguish the formation from line of battle. The order of march had been the same since they left Wark the previous week. The leading battalion was the vanguard (from the French *avant garde*), the formation with the most intrinsic prestige in the army. The vanguard would be first in battle should the army meet another on the road, and their position when deployed in line for battle would be correspondingly dangerous. This vanguard contained the Earls of Hereford and Gloucester, John Comyn (son of the Red Comyn), King Edward's steward, as well as other famous and experienced knights. Following the vanguard came the main body of troops, including eight battalions of horsemen. As well, the main body contained the foot soldiers: billmen, archers and knifemen all, the richer ones mounted but most walking, guarded and kept in line by constables on horseback.

As the army approached Stirling it entered the forest of the Tor Wood. The combination of woods and uneven terrain made it difficult to see more than a few yards in any direction except for front and back. The wagon drivers and guards could no longer expect any warning of attack, when the Scots could approach in the cover of the trees.

In farming country, the army could spread out over the fields to either side of the road. In wooded country, this was not feasible. The verge of the road, close to the trees, from which an attack would come, was the most dangerous place to march. The more nervous soldiers would gravitate to the centre of the road. Most of the men had to leave the road at some point during the march, find a tree or ditch to do his business, then run to catch up with his comrades. The same procedure was difficult for the knights, who needed to stop and dismount in order to do the same thing, but it was not impossible. The verges of the road were occasionally confused with knights and men rejoining their friends as well as couriers carrying messages between the vanguard, the king and the rear guard.

At the rear of the main body, in the last main battalion of cavalry, rode the king and his party. The king's party included the royal banner and the knights detailed to hold the royal reins and the royal shield. Separate knights were needed to hold the reins, so that should the king be endangered he could be taken from the field without the stigma of having left of his own volition. None could call the king a coward when he had to be dragged from the field, and the kingdom need not fear the ruinous ransom that would surely be exacted should the king be captured. In this case Aylmer de Valence, Earl of Pembroke, and Sir Giles de Argentine had forgone their places in the vanguard for the duty of attending the king, one on each rein.

Also with the king were his heralds and those of his earls, in their tabards painted or embroidered with the arms of their employers. The king's heralds wore red coats emblazoned with the three leopards (in the language of heralds, a leopard is a sort of lion) that had grown out of Richard the Lionheart's two-lion shield. These were specialists in the technicalities of war. They understood the differences between the arms on the knights' heraldic surcoats (these garments were literally coats of arms), and the niceties of parleys with the enemy. They knew the rules of war and of single combat. As recognised neutrals (though they often went armoured) they carried messages between the commanders of either side. In a campaign between chivalric opponents the heralds helped orchestrate the knightly phases of the battles, from the opening challenges to the declaration of victory and the naming of the battle at the end. The heralds would be little employed on this expedition.

In a campaign against a guerrilla army like Bruce's, the wagon train was the most vulnerable part of the army. An attack from the side of the road would avoid the strong vanguard, so the wagons were driven with soldiers to either side to protect them. The space this required drew the wagon train out over a long stretch of road indeed. One would hope, for the sake of the infantrymen, that the wagons went behind them and not before. By the time a stretch of road had been passed over by all the horses of the cavalry and the teamsters as well as the carters' oxen, dropping manure as they went, there could be no doubt to any observer that an army had passed. While this surface would be nothing new to an English or Welsh peasant whose livestock were penned in his living room, this sort of pavement would hardly be conducive to happy or comfortable marching.

The last battalion of horse, the rear guard, followed the wagon train. In the event of an attack from the rear, this battalion would engage the enemy. While the rear guard fought and cried the alarm, the rest of the army would have time to turn and prepare.

As they advanced, the English were indeed observed. A scouting party under the command of Keith the Marshal spent the morning patrolling the road through the woods, waiting for the English. When they saw the bright banners and polished helmets of the English knights, their lances a bright forest blossoming with pennons, they turned back to tell King Robert. Here Dean Barbour tells us that the advancing English looked like angels (he says this on more than one occasion). This is a Latin pun on Angles looking like angels (and after Pope Gregory the Great was the first to crack this line seven hundred years before, it achieved the character of a cliché description of Englishmen). King Robert decided that it was inappropriate to tell his men that they would be facing an angelic host in battle, and so he had his messengers go to the various battalions and tell them that the English were sloping down the road in clumsy disarray. After all, when several thousand pounds of sharp, spiked, armoured horseflesh and knightflesh come barrelling at the gallop, and survival depends on the men not breaking ranks in panic, there can be no over-confidence.

The Plantagenet's army marched through the forest. As they marched, the signs of the Scottish army became more apparent. Robert Bruce had stayed with his army in this wood for a month, and there were cold fireplaces, garbage pits, empty barrels and broken crockery to mark each camp. At this first tangible evidence of the Scots army a feeling of foreboding came upon the common soldiers. While knights generally survived battles, unscathed or captured and ransomed, foot soldiers were killed in droves. Even if their barons won the battle, it was often the common soldier who would foot the butcher's bill. Those lucky enough only to be wounded could look forward to the agony of infection, often leading to death.

From Falkirk to the end of the Tor Wood, within sight of Stirling Castle, was a morning's march. It was one or two hours past noon when the vanguard saw the light at the end of the woods. There, coming down the road, was a knight with his retainers. The Earls of Gloucester and Hereford recognised by the knight's surcoat and banner that he was Philip de Mowbray, the governor of Stirling Castle. They let him hasten past with a wave.

Mowbray raced past the vanguard and the first battalions of the main force, pulling his horse up at the great red silk banner painted with the three gold leopards of Anjou. Armed with a safe conduct from King Robert, he had ridden through the New Park and through the Scottish army there, pursued by the jeers of the Scottish soldiery, and he had news for King Edward.

Riding alongside the king, the governor offered congratulations on arriving within three leagues of Stirling Castle in time to relieve the garrison. Now that the Plantagenet was here, one year to the day from the bargain Mowbray had executed with Edward Bruce, the siege was lifted and the castle need not be surrendered. Now the ships from Edinburgh could sail upriver and re-supply the garrison. The king need proceed no further.

Several hundred yards away the English vanguard came out of the woods. Across a small valley broken by the

Bannockburn, just outside a place where the road entered the New Forest, they saw a small troop of knights mounted on light horses, and behind them a troop of foot soldiers. Snapping over their heads was a yellow silk banner emblazoned with the scarlet lion of Scotland. At the head of the English vanguard, Gilbert de Clare, Earl of Gloucester, who had been appointed constable of the army by King Edward, suggested that he ought to lead the charge against the enemy. Beside him Humphrey de Bohun, Earl of Hereford, hereditary constable of England, said he wouldn't hear of it. Bohuns have always led English charges, he said, and a Bohun would lead this one.

King Edward, still engaged in conversation with Philip de Mowbray, was not interested in the technicalities of the relief of Stirling. He had come to chase the rebel Bruce to the ground and destroy his army. The relief and re-supply of his fortress on Stirling Rock was only a pretext to come to Scotland, and a welcome dividend of the expedition. The king asked Mowbray what lay ahead.

Mowbray reported that the road was blocked all the way through the woods by four schiltrons of infantry and a battalion of light horse. The side paths were blocked with felled trees. The verges of the road were mined, he said, and if they advanced it would be another Loudon, with the English trapped on a narrow front, dying in ignominious defeat against Scottish infantry. The Earl of Pembroke harrumphed. Pembroke had commanded the English army at Loudon. Very well, said King Edward, he would call a halt while they decided what to do.

The Earl of Hereford pricked his spurs into his horse, tipped his helmet shut, and fixed his lance, his friends and retainers following. The Earl of Gloucester, not to be out-done, brought up his shield and galloped alongside. Henry de Bohun, Hereford's nephew, saw Gloucester pulling ahead and determined that the Bohun name must be preserved against that of Clare. He spurred his horse on, running out ahead of the rivals, splashing through the wide, shallow ford in the burn. He rode at a hand gallop, the pace at which the horse is just short of galloping out of control.

The king of England's battalion halted, and the battalions ahead in the main force were stopped by a constable. Another constable rode to stop the vanguard before it got too far ahead. When he got to the front of the main body of the army, halted there on the road, the constable looked around for the vanguard. It wasn't there. He asked the knights of the front battalion where the vanguard had gone. They pointed their gauntleted hands ahead, at the break in the trees.

Keith the marshal was just back from his reconnaissance, and King Robert had gone out to meet him. They sat their horses out in front of their troop of cavalry and looked with wonder on the oncoming English. Robert could hardly believe his good fortune. That Pembroke would make the same mistake he had made at Loudon – it was all he had hoped for. Only a few more yards and the knights would be between the minefields, and he would send his spears in. Keith started moving the horsemen of the reconnaissance party back behind the foot soldiers.

Henry de Bohun could not believe his good fortune. Not only was a Bohun leading the charge, as was proper, but there, across the field, was the king of Scots, golden crown on his helmet and silk banner at his back. What a prize this would be, to kill his king's arch-enemy; what a way to royal favour. And there the Bruce was, mounted on a small grey palfrey, not even on a proper destrier. It almost wasn't fair. Almost.

King Robert trotted out ahead of his standing soldiers, hefting his axe in his hand. Killing knights was work for a sword, but axe he had and axe he would use to fell this English oak. Bruce held his pony still, gentling her with his gloved left hand. As Bohun rumbled closer, his kin spurring on behind, Bruce took a firm grip with both hands on the timber of his axe-haft. When the tip of Bohun's lance was a horse's-length away and the thunder of his charger's hooves carried to Bruce through his stirrups, he nudged his pony with a boot.

Henry de Bohun knew something was wrong. He had ranged the Scottish king well, yet he had not felt the guard of his lance smash against his shoulder armour with the impact of collision. He raised his head, the better to see ahead through his eye-slits, and Bruce wasn't there.

Robert the Bruce, his horse off to Henry's side, stood in his stirrups and twisted to his right, winding up to swing his axe. Just as Bohun's head came up, Bruce twisted back. He swung his axe like a lumberman, his right hand sliding along the hardwood of the haft to meet his left.

Out of the corner of his eye, Bohun saw the gold of Bruce's crown glitter as the Scottish king spun around. The axe struck downwards against the edge of Bohun's visor, with all the force of Bruce's arms, and the force of his torso as he swung around with the blow. Add to that the momentum of Bohun's mass, galloping at fifty kilometres per hour, and the result was the axe crushing the visor and helmet out of the way, cutting right through the gap and into the Englishman's head, cleaving it almost in two. The late Henry de Bohun's horse kept moving, its gory cargo lurching in the saddle. As the Bruce twisted his axe free he saw that the axe-haft was broken, cracked all along its length and held together only by the iron head.

Meanwhile, in the main body of the vanguard, the Earl of Gloucester moved his horse aside, away from the road. Family pride had to take a back seat to charging on a wide front and thus maximising the effect of the attack. He felt a sudden lurch and a drop, and then he was flying through the air, landing with a painful thump, spreadeagled on the ground. The minefields had claimed their first important victim.

Humphrey de Bohun had seen his brother's boy cut down. He had seen his rival's horse plunge into a pitfall and he had seen the spears coming from the woods. He realised that this was a trap, and bellowed to his fellows to retreat. As they slowed their horses and fought them around in tight circles, the knights in the rear barrelling into the ones in front and cursing in confusion, they heard the cries of the Scots infantrymen who were descending the gentle slope to the burn. The knights rode their horses away, back into the woods. There they turned again and prepared to charge down the valley at their enemy when they crossed the burn, away from the minefields. From the cover of the woods they saw the Scots, held back by their sergeants, waving from across the valley: that, and Gilbert de Clare, the proud Earl of Gloucester, shield on his back and helmet under his arm, running up the slope and blaspheming roundly.

Keith and the other Scottish nobles who were near King Robert's battalion came to congratulate their king. With their kudos came a word of reproach. He ought not to have endangered himself that way, putting his little grey pony in the way of a fully horsed and armoured knight. After all, if the Bruce died then the Scottish kingdom died with him. Robert's reply: he broke my axe.

The king of England had not heard of the engagement. He still sat his horse on the Roman road, deciding what to do. He consulted his friends, and resolved to send a reconnaissance in force. He dispatched Lord Clifford, one of his experienced bannerets, to explore the way around the wood through Stirling carse. Perhaps he also meant them to block the Scots from retreating or from otherwise menacing the castle. The rest of the army would wait on the road in the Tor Wood.

Lord Clifford took his battalion slowly through the wood to the east. Once they had cleared the edge of the trees, the battalion rode down the slope to the carse. They forded the Bannockburn where it flowed forth from its cut in the hill, and keeping the Scot-infested woods far to the left they cantered across the foot of the slope towards Stirling Castle in the distance.

King Robert sat his horse on the edge of the wood. There the message came to him, borne hot-foot by a scout. A party of horsemen was fording the burn, he said: one battalion of them. King Robert sent word to Thomas Randolph, the Earl of Moray, whose battalion of foot soldiers was closest to the castle. A rose had fallen from King Robert's wreath, read the message (the wreath of his victory over the vanguard). Moray's orders were to retrieve the rose. Moray acted quickly, ordering his men out of the woods. Each man sought his buddy as he jogged down the grade, and when they reached the bottom of the hill they formed their schiltron.

The Black Douglas saw the Moraymen running to stop Clifford's foray. He begged King Robert to be allowed to take Walter the Steward's battalion along, to help Moray against the horse. Robert said no; the English on the road in the Tor Wood were a threat, and the troop or two of horse commanded by Clifford did not merit committing two of his four battalions to the fight.

Sir Henry Beaumont rode beside Lord Clifford, and when Moray's spears began to trot down the hill by St Ninian's Kirk, Beaumont suggested that instead of charging uphill they wait until they could engage the Scots on the flat. Lord Clifford stopped his men there, and they watched as the mob of soldiers formed their wall round about their sergeants, the outer rank kneeling. Then Lord Clifford closed his visor and raised his shield. The knights set spurs to their horses and lowered their lances.

The knights at the front of the battalion were William Deyncourt and Thomas Gray. Their chargers were egged on by the other stallions' hoofbeats, and soon the horses were galloping out of control. When the first horses struck the Moray spears they reared up, screaming. They twisted aside and around, forcing the other horses to turn aside, though some must have stumbled and pushed Gray's and Deyncourt's horses into the spears' range. The spearmen set their points against the joints in armour and leaned their weight into the thrusts. Deyncourt was killed, by spears or by a bad fall. Gray was pulled within the schiltron and taken prisoner, later to be ransomed. The rest of the battalion turned their mounts aside, and rode away from the schiltron to gain fighting room.

The knights charged and charged again, turning aside when the pikes remained unmoved. When one came too close, a standing spearman of the inner ring ran forward and stabbed at him. The sergeants within the ring pulled the eager spearmen back, shouting at the soldiers to hold their formation. So long as the hedge of iron points did not break, the soldiers would be safe from the knights' lances.

The English saw that their lances were useless against the long pikes, their swords more so. They began to throw their maces and flails at the Scots (though their swords were too expensive to use that way), but they got little satisfaction. Whenever a lucky shot put a pikeman down, senseless or with a nasty bruise, another would be dispatched from within the ring to fill his mate's place. The Scottish sergeants made a pile of the weapons in the middle of the schiltron, and continued to bellow at their men in a tradition of shouting inherited from the Roman centurions and from their predecessors before them.

King Robert finally gave in to the Black Douglas's entreaties. Perhaps his scouts brought word that the English had stopped in the woods, and after the repulse of the English vanguard, Robert was feeling cocky enough to pit half of his army against a tenth of King Edward's. He gave Douglas permission to bring his battalion down the hill to help the Earl of Moray. By the time the men came to the edge of the hill, however, it was apparent to Douglas that the schiltron had held for a long time, and that it was not about to break. If his battalion joined in he would be risking his troops for no reason, and should his own troops be less adept than Moray's at maintaining their formation, the risk would be all the greater. Also, Moray had done the work of rushing to do battle and forming up quickly. His sergeants and men had done their job well, and it would have been unfair to force Moray to share the glory of victory. So the Black Douglas held his men there at the top of the hill.

The English horsemen did not know that Douglas would not come down the hill. They saw another troop of spears, looking down the hill at them, and realised that even if they could break into the first schiltron, another would come down after them. Indeed, from the foot of the slope they were unable to see much of the top of the hill, so they could not have assumed that only Stewart's battalion stood ready to attack; it might have been the entire Scottish army. Clifford called his men off, and waved them back the way they had come. Some might have gone off to Stirling Castle, in order to reinforce with their armed presence the token relief effected by the proximity of the English army. Clifford, however, turned his horse back towards the Tor Wood in order to report to the king on this engagement.

If Clifford was attempting to take his troop to Stirling, then he can be faulted for not having taken advantage of the speed of his horses to outrun the Scottish foot soldiers to the castle, and in that case his foray was a miserable failure. If he was attempting to make a reconnaissance in force, to scout out the carse as a suitable route to the castle, then his operation was something of a success. From the encounter, Clifford learned that the Scots could deploy easily down the hill, forming quickly at the bottom. He learned that the schiltrons were virtually impervious to cavalry attack (which other English knights might have remembered from Falkirk), even without the chains and timbers that Wallace had used to reinforce them. On the non-tactical side, Clifford discovered that there was high, dry ground on the carse, and that the dry portion would be suitable for camping that night and marching the next day.

Some would say that even if Clifford understood the tactical lessons he had been taught by the Earl of Moray, his superiors did not. Once again, the assumption is that King Edward was a fool, and ignored Moray's success. More likely, however, is the possibility that King Edward prepared the next day with the Clifford engagement in mind. The next morning he deployed his troops with groups of archers on either flank, the better to pepper the schiltrons with arrows. On the other hand, he could not be faulted for believing that while King Robert might send a quarter of his army to attack one isolated battalion of English horse, he would not commit his entire army to an open-field encounter with the entire English army. It just was not the Bruce's way of fighting.

8

The Carse and the New Park

Night of 23/24 June 1314

The poor condemnèd English,
Like sacrifices, by their watchful fires,
Sit patiently, and inly ruminate
The morning's danger;

King Henry V, William Shakespeare

The Crossing

The army of Edward II had just completed a long march through Lauderdale to Edinburgh and thence to the Tor Wood. The soldiers had stopped, standing in the June sun for hours, only to hear that the proud horsemen of the vanguard had been routed by the Bruce. Now the constables sent word down the line that the army would turn aside.

A modern historian described the subsequent manoeuvre blithely. He said the English army 'must wheel at once to the right', and march parallel to the Bannockburn. His military frame of reference is obviously that of the modern drill ground rather than that of a large army that had no term for 'wheel'. A modern line of soldiers wheels right by means of the man on the right end of the line, the pivot, standing still or 'marking time' by marching in place while the man on the left end of the line marches with long strides in a ninety-degree arc to the right. The soldiers in the middle maintain line abreast, thus the entire line acts like a spoke of a wheel. This manoeuvre requires practice and drill to accomplish, and that with only one line. To wheel an entire army, with row after row of soldiers turning precisely, so that the column of men never stops moving or even slows down, takes a great deal of practice indeed. This sort of Prussian drill-ground acrobatics started to become important in the sixteenth century, the age of pike and gun squares. There is no evidence to suggest that armies of the fourteenth century (especially armies filled with undisciplined Welsh knifemen) even attempted to exercise this sort of order.

In order to take an army which filled a north-south road for half a mile, and bring it across the Bannockburn at a safe distance from the Scots in the wood, the English had to move east and north several hundred yards where there was no road. A foot-path or cart-track wide enough to permit the passage of the folk of Bannockburn Town on their way to Dere Street for whatever reason would hardly have been wide enough to ease the passage of several hundred warhorses, palfreys, remounts and pack horses and a thousand foot, as well as the oxen and goods wagons necessary to the provisioning of the army.

The army must have oozed from the road, each group of comrades-in-arms taking the easiest way across the fields and through the woods near Bannockburn Town to the ford there. The horsemen and the carters took the townsfolk's tracks while the ordinary soldier made his way as best he could, the men at the front turning right and walking along the burn while the men at the rear, half a mile or so behind, struck out through copses and across emptied pastures for the town in the distance. Each small group of friends would certainly have tried to take the shortest path to the town, rather than attempt some aesthetic, geometric turning at right angles. Many gravitated to St Peter's Well on the heights overlooking the carse, and took a drink before moving along.

The crossing began when the first groups of horsemen arrived at the ford. The horses picked their way through the wide, relatively shallow waters. The stream itself presented little difficulty for the horses, considering that the crossing was far upstream from the tidal bog, and the fast-flowing burn cleaned mud and silt quickly, without allowing it to turn the bottom to muck. So long as the horses had leisure to pick their way over stones and around holes in the bottom, the crossing was safe and quick. When the infantry began to arrive at the ford some crossed further upstream and some further down, taking advantage of Man's superiority to horse in nimbleness and flexibility. Some twisted their ankles, and some fell in for a good soaking. All, however, had forded other burns in the last few days' march. This was not a new experience for anyone.

The chroniclers tell us that Bannockburn Town was at least partially dismantled to provide bridging materials, and even that the castle garrison brought more stuff from Stirling Town. The usual explanation is that the English bridged the Bannockburn to camp in the Polls, crossing either at the wide, muddy-bottomed lower reaches of the burn, where it spills into the Forth, or at the ravine through which the burn flows swift and deep. Those who theorise that the English camped in the bog of the Polls overnight also accept that the thatch and timber of the town was used to cover over streams and tidal pools so that the horses could cross easily. This version would have English sappers spend the entire afternoon and evening building bridges over pows, bridges that would surely not be reliable, just so that the army could spend the night in an evil bog and march across it in the day. If, however, the English commanders preferred to sleep on dry ground (as most people would), and cross at a wide ford rather than a narrow, makeshift bridge, the dismantling is more of a mystery. If the army avoided the marshy Polls (which is likely considering that their lengthy crossing probably included evening high tide), and crossed to the carse further upstream, what could they be bridging? Surely not the Bannockburn. Why take the time and effort to bridge the burn when it could be forded? Horses have little trouble slowly negotiating fords. Indeed, steeplechasers prove that a horse can be jumped into a stream and ridden out the other side with only a few going down – and that at breakneck speed. Men have even less trouble than horses, once they are convinced to get wet, and on a warm June afternoon after several days' hard march, the cool, spring-fed waters of the Bannockburn must not have seemed unwelcome.

Real bridging, while a possibility, is unlikely. It does not seem conceivable that the entire English army stood still by a shallow ford while some sappers lashed door-frames together to make a dry span, nor would it be tactically sound for a commander to sacrifice a crossing in broad ranks in favour of squeezing across a bridge. It is unlikely that they would have benefited from making a broad dam of thatch and timber and trying to get several hundred horses to negotiate it without breaking legs, while the waters of the stream rushed over and through.

The engineering might well have been in order to facilitate the crossing, rather than actually bridge the Polls or the burns. One horse fording a stream makes for a great deal of splashing and dripping on the bank once across. One horse can turn some of the ground on the far side to mud, and can churn the mud with its hooves. A hundred horses can turn a once-dry crossing place into an uncomfortable swamp. Several hundred horses' hooves churning several hundred horses' splashings into the dirt will create a morass impassable to ox- and horse-carts. The absorbent reeds of thatch from Bannockburn Town, laid on the mud in bundles, turned the loose muck of the banks into a thick, fibrous mortar, with some purchase for men and pack animals. The addition of timbers from the houses made the banks of the ford into a sort of corduroy road, with the thatch-mud combination acting as cement between the baulks.

In their crossings before reaching Tor Wood, when the army forded a stream without the pressure of a nearby enemy, they could send their horses, men and carts across at different places along a wide section of stream. As such, they need not have broken up towns in this way until now, when a few yards' ford was all they could use.

Further reinforcement might have been necessary at the banks of the Pel Stream, which flows about halfway between the ford at Bannockburn Town and the bridge at Stirling, and the smaller streams which cut across the high ground of the carse to feed into the Polls. This would allow the English to cross briskly in the morning without breaking battle order.

The Camp

The officers in charge of determining an army's stopping place for the night were called harbingers. Among the first English horsemen to whip their horses up the banks of the Bannockburn were these harbingers, and they set about finding a place for the king, for the knights and incidentally for the rest of the soldiers. The choice of campsite was governed by three primary considerations: first, safety from enemy surprise attack; second, access from the ford and to Stirling; third, comfort.

The safety factor was especially important since the woods overlooking the carse contained several hundred Scotsmen with murder in their eyes. The English could not observe the Scots. King Robert Bruce's army had the advantage of tree cover, protecting them not only from English eyes but from English scouts on horseback. In addition, the New Park grew on a steep bluff overlooking the carse, rendering the Scots virtually invisible from below. So the English needed a campground close enough to Stirling to make it an easy morning's march to the castle, but far enough from the New Park that if howling northerners came rushing down the bluff in the middle of the night, the English would have time to pull their pants on and defend themselves.

The harbingers did not choose a place too near the ford, since muddy oxen and their muddy wagons were being hauled up the banks there. Indeed, several hundred horses and their riders, several hundred soldiers and tens of carts and their oxen all emerging from a cold dunking to find themselves all on the same bank and in need of direction must have been a scene of remarkable chaos, with constables

trying to whip the men into order with their batons, screaming at those who wandered in the wrong direction. The harbingers did not want to set their camp up in the midst of this
disorder.

The tidal bog of the Polls cannot have impressed them as
a comfortable place to spend the night, and the upper carse,
towards the wood, was too dangerous for its proximity to the
Scots. The lower carse, at least fifty yards from the ford, was
the best place to camp. There was room for the soldiers and
teamsters to get to their feet and sort themselves out, as well
as room for a deep screen of pickets between them and their
enemy.

Comfort is, of course, a relative term. The harbingers took
this into account when they chose campgrounds. There had
to be high, firm ground for the pavilions of the king and the
earls. There needed to be firm ground all around, for their
horses and their servants and their field kitchen. The pavilions
were not closely packed. Each magnate wanted room enough
for himself and his men, and privacy of sight and sound from
his brother peers.

Those lesser knights who had tents and wagons also needed high, firm ground. There was armour and tack to be dried
carefully and oiled after the dunking in the burn. There was
the next day's march to prepare for and the harbingers knew
it was the rare knight who would willingly do that work
while up to his chin in a bog, risking his horses breaking their
legs in mud-holes. So there had to be hard ground for the
earls and knights, and enough of it that the traffic of wagons
could pass and be unloaded. As such it is hardly conceivable
that they marched the extra mile to make their camp in a
swamp, as some writers would have us believe.

There was no need to find ground for the common soldiers' tents, because the common soldiers had no tents. Barracks tents for the infantry grunt were centuries in the future, and unless he and his group of comrades could evict a local peasant family and their livestock from their hut, the soldier would have the pleasure, as later generations esteemed it, of 'sleeping under the stars'. The more enterprising and energetic groups built lean-tos roofed with straw or stolen thatch. Some found a bush or a tree to shield them from the elements, but most wrapped themselves up in their cloaks and dossed down on a comfortable hummock. All were liable to get nasty colds from sleeping on the ground with only thin protection underneath, and they had bivouacked like this every night for the past several weeks, ever since they had left their villages. Many of them suffered from vicious summer colds, on top of the allergies which must have been inflamed by the unfamiliar pollen of Scotland.

Once the horse and the wagons had got across the burn, and the order was given to make camp, many of the soldiers who had been at the back of the column on the road, and who were only just arriving at the ford, must have decided not to bother crossing. There need not have been an executive decision to keep a large proportion of the English foot soldiers to the far side of the burn from Stirling: the weariness of two days' brisk march is enough to convince a man to take his rest where he stands without an officer telling him so. There was no particular reason to bring them across, as most of them were Welsh foot soldiers and archers who were useful in a large brawl on rough ground, but who were not much good in a threatening military parade. They would be used later as hounds to hunt Bruce the Carrick fox and his army. The English archers had to be got across, however, since they had proved their usefulness at Falkirk against Scottish schiltrons.

Although it was many hours after noon, the sun had not set. It was, after all, high summer in Scotland, when the sun sets late in the evening and the afternoon is nine hours long. This was just as well, since there was a great deal of work to be done. Even the servants who were on their first campaign had been making and breaking camp every night since leaving Wark, and every few nights since their lords had left their own houses, so the work was accomplished quickly. Also, the great men and the knights had squires to look after their horses and armour. Even the lesser horsemen needed to look after their mounts and equipment, the tools of their trade.

After a hot day's work carrying a man in armour, a horse needs a good brushing and light exercise, before a thorough watering and feeding. These considerations are far from finicky aesthetic points. If the sequence is not followed properly, a horse will die, and the death of a horse was an unacceptable loss of capital equipment.

Squires attended to the armour, which could begin to rust overnight if it was not dried properly and oiled against further moisture. Chain mail is particularly difficult to clean. Some of the knights took off the sweaty padding which underlay their armour, and hung it out to dry in the evening air, perhaps on racks of lances. If a knight had a spare padded jack, he donned it soon and buckled the armour on again, for the dark line of trees on the brow of the bluff reminded him that the Scots lurked nearby. Nobody wanted to be caught unarmoured if the Scots roared out of the woods in one of their notorious guerrilla raids. Once the first lot of horses had been brushed, rubbed, exercised and watered, they were re-harnessed. Their riders slipped their bits loose so that they could graze, and the knights stood or sat nearby, relieving the mounts of their weight. They grumbled to one another about aching knees and the fatigue of riding, and traded grim stories with their fellows about the great hedgehog of pikes that had laughed at Clifford, and about the ill-fated charge of Henry de Bohun.

Henry's uncle, Humphrey, by virtue of being Earl of Hereford and Essex, was probably not keeping nervous watch all night. Hereford's travelling household had just two days before received a new supply of food from his ship anchored at Edinburgh, so bread and wine were plentiful (it was a religious fast day, so the Earl probably eschewed meat). He and his friends sat in chairs, their feet up on tables, and discussed the late Henry, who had sat with them only the night before. Some might have said that the young knight was a fool for charging recklessly into the Scots host, but most toasted his bravery and his splendid death, worthy of a hero of chivalric legend. After all, of the companions who had shared the Earl of Hereford's bread the previous night, the only one history remembers is the nephew who shivered Robert Bruce's axe-haft with his face.

As they sat there with their food and wine, their horses, like the horses of the other earls and their friends and the king's horses, were fed not on the coarse, dry June grass of the carse, but on meal brought from the supply-ships in Edinburgh. If they were fed only the meal, and not a liberal amount of the meadow grass for additional roughage, then they would be high-strung and skittish the next day. Far from being undesirable, these qualities were mistaken for fierceness and prized in warhorses. Indeed, all the cavalry who could afford to ride a stallion did so, and the worse-tempered and more 'fiery' the horse the better. Only in later ages were geldings and mares preferred by horse soldiers, when a cavalryman's ability as a 'team player' became more important than his (and his horse's) individual fierceness. So the earls and their friends instructed the grooms to restrict the horses' grazing in order that the beasts might snort and kick all the more on the morrow.

When the king's friends sat down to their dinner, they talked about the next day's march. Unlike the march along the Roman street, strung out only as wide as the road, in a column that could be stopped and damaged by surprise attacks along the flanks, the next day's exercise would be a march in force, deployed broadly over the field, their archers on their flanks in the formation that had won Edward's father so many battles in Wales. They would be unopposed, they knew, for in previous years no Scottish army had opposed an English army in the field. The march in force was to drive home to Bruce and his friends, and to those Scottish barons whose loyalties wavered, the point that Edward Plantagenet was king of a unified British kingdom, and no forsworn chieftain with a rout of ragged rebels was going to say him nay. The march would serve to wipe away the stain of Clifford's and Bohun's encounters. If there was some opposition on their march across the carse to Stirling, it could be swept aside by the might of English chivalry. After all, an entire Edwardian army was more powerful by orders of magnitude than Clifford's scouting party or Bohun's vanguard.

At the king's table, the Earl of Gloucester, constable of the army, swallowed hard and prepared to say something unpopular. He suggested that since Stirling Castle was technically relieved, the army ought to remain camped for the following day (a saint's day, after all) in order to regain their strength after their long, brisk march. He reasoned that they would have several days' marching ahead of them, as they chased and fought the Bruce's army, and some rest would do them good. The earl was, however, trying to sell to the wrong crowd. Sitting with the king at the table was the Earl of Pembroke as well as Hugh Despenser, Giles de Argentine, Robert Clifford and others: a group of professional knights to whom an army was a group of chivalric brethren with the peasants along to watch. Sir Giles de Argentine, ransomed from the Byzantine Emperor for this campaign and brought over from Constantinople, was a paragon of knightly virtue, to whom the idea of resting an army near live foemen was foreign. Those of less suicidally brave spirit than Argentine might also have thought of how nice it would be to sleep the next night safe within the walls of Stirling Castle, with their soldiers cantoned in Stirling Town and the villages round about, in a military barrier that Robert Bruce could not break. Some recalled the rumours that Gloucester had sent his gift of spurs to warn Bruce to flee the court of the king's father, and thus had preserved the rebel Earl of Carrick to worry them that night. Gloucester was chaffed at, and even his cousin the king called him a traitor and a coward for his advice.

Neither the king's companions, nor the earls, nor their servants, nor the horsemen and footmen who sat in the waning light of evening took any notice of a horse picking its way around bivouacked soldiers, racked lances and drowsing pickets, to the outermost reaches of the English camp. No moon hung in the sky to light his passage. There, with none to stop him, he spurred his horse across the carse and up the bluff into the New Park.

> What a wretched and peevish fellow is this king of
> England, to mope with his fat-brained followers so far
> out of his knowledge!

King Henry V, William Shakespeare

New Park

In the cool fastness of the forest, King Robert's army was full of jubilation. First the news of Henry de Bohun's death at the hands of the Scottish king had spread like wildfire from Bruce's own battalion to those of his kinsmen and friends. Each soldier must have repeated to his mates King Robert's lament over the crack of his axe-haft. The story of the English vanguard running from ignominious defeat flew through the ranks next; each man who was there lamented that he had not been allowed to pursue the fleeing foe.

After the brief anxiety as Moray's battalion hustled to meet Clifford's horse, the Stewart's men on the bluff had been treated to the sight of English horsemen shaking their swords and fists in frustration as a schiltron held fast. No doubt they cheered each time an English knight ventured too close and was pulled within the wall of pikes. No doubt they laughed each time a frustrated Englishman threw his mace into the Scottish hedgehog. When Clifford's troop finally turned away in disgust the cheers of the Scots turned to roars of delight as soldiers pounded each other on the back and crowed over their enemies' shame.

As the English army began to move off the Roman road and make for the fording place, the Scots began to pack up their cooking plates and bags of oats for the trip to their next encampment in Lennox, where they could hit a following English army with greater strength. The Scots had nothing further to do to the English here. They were a guerrilla army and their job was to strike hard and run quickly. They had made the English pay heavily from their store of pride for the return of Stirling Castle, and now they would leave, living to lay siege once again when Edward's attentions were elsewhere, just as Wallace and Bruce had done with Edward's father.

The Scottish lookouts sat on the brow of the bluff, watching the English begin their fording operation. They were hardly worried about an English surprise attack. The English horse would have had to charge up a broad field in plain view, gallop up a long grade and then attempt to ride their horses in the forest while killing people (people who were uninterested in being killed, and who were therefore fighting back): a possible but fruitless exercise. They sat in the shade, munching on bannocks and drinking water from the cold spring at St Ninian's Kirk. Although the cook-fires might have been kept within the cover of the wood, the telltale smoke told the English that, at least for the moment, their enemies watched and waited. Once night fell, the Scots could depart in safety, leaving the English a few hours' confusion as to which way the army had gone.

Night fell late at Stirling, north of the 56th parallel of north latitude. Sunset came eight hours and forty-eight minutes after local noon: at 22:03 British Summer Time (BST), if they'd had such a thing (which they hadn't). Because the sun didn't go far below the horizon in the Scottish midsummer, it never got fully dark. It was 'nautical twilight', in modern terms, from sunset until the sun rose just before 04:27 BST the next day. Just under six and a half hours of semidarkness.

In the uncertain illumination of twilight one of the lookouts saw an armoured figure riding along the Pelstream Burn and up the hill to the wood, hunched over his saddle. The fact that the rider was alone kept the Scots officers from assuming that this was an attack, and they sounded no general alarm. The rider was met by the hostile faces of armed men, and he was escorted to Dere Street, where Robert the Bruce held court.

A council of war is at base a forum for a general to inform his subordinates of his plans and orders for an upcoming event, and to consult with them. Different levels of consultation and counsel can take place, depending on the general, his subordinates, his political position relative to his subordinates and his military competence relative to his subordinates. A strong commander of no great competence might consult his subordinates heavily just as a weak commander, whatever his skills as a general, might need to accept advice or direction from his theoretical subordinates.

Here King Robert, general of an army comprising various elements of a divided Scotland, needed at least to give his confederates the illusion that they were being consulted. After all, should a leader not be satisfied that his interests and his men's were being served, they could easily melt away into the night, back to their homes and farms or across the carse to the English camp. Thus it was not a small circle of Robert's intimates that met in the wood, but representatives from all the clans, companies, lordships and lairdships that made up the Scottish army.

King Robert had learned the hard way that the guerrilla warfare made successful by Wallace was the only way a Scottish army could inflict damage on an English army. The woods were filled with an army of his supporters, but the surest way to defeat and the imprisonment of more of his friends and family was to meet the English on an open field of battle.

He had set up a battle for himself to win. It was to have been like the Battle of Loudon Hill, with the English advancing on a narrow front bordered by pitfalls, there to be lacerated by Scottish spears. It was to have taken place on the Roman road, at the Entry. Unfortunately, it had taken place that afternoon, and in only a few minutes the English had been sent packing with next to no casualties on either side. If he fought tomorrow, the certainties he had built into the Entry would be gone, and it would be (so to speak) a whole new ball game.

Certainly the schiltron formation that his men had practised that spring in the Tor Wood was useful. It had certainly frustrated Clifford's sally earlier that day. But Clifford's troop had been one battalion on a reconnaissance in force, whereas across the carse was an entire army. He had told his men that the enemy advanced in disorder, but he had seen the rows of polished helmets and fluttering pennons amidst the forest of lances. He knew that he faced an Edwardian army of the sort that had won Wales and had humiliated him and captured or killed his brothers, his sister, his wife, his daughter and his friends.

King Robert the Bruce was ready to cash in his chips and head for the Lennox hills with his winnings. No doubt some of his commanders were willing to do the same. They knew that once Edward's feudal host melted away in late summer the Scots could return and retake Stirling. They knew that each time Edward gathered an army it would either be smaller or more expensive than the last. They knew that the English barons did not approve of this campaign, and should King Edward return with nothing but the death of Bohun and the rout of Clifford to add to the relief of Stirling, they would hardly approve of the next campaign.

Other commanders were less interested in the long-term political goal of a Bruce rather than Plantagenet Scotland. They wanted the booty that a battle would bring. They wanted their pick of the enemy's horses and the enemy's plate. Some of them were downright bloodthirsty and wanted nothing more than to drive spears into Englishmen and Welshmen, not to mention Badenoch men. These were not only sentiments one might find in a highland chieftain, but just as likely in a Frenchified lowland knight, who depended on military victory for a significant portion of his income.

Into this council was brought Sir Alexander Seton, the Scottish knight who had ridden from the English lines in the twilight. He was just as much a Scotsman as Robert de Brus, who had held the earldom of Carrick in fief of King Edward I, but Seton had chosen to side with the English in this war. Now he had turned his coat and come from the Plantagenet camp with advice for King Robert, a deed for which he would one day be made the Bruce's deputy seneschal.

The English were demoralised, he said. Robert should join battle with them on the morrow, and he would be victorious. Cut off my head and pull out my guts if it isn't so, he swore. This we know he said. He might also have told King Robert the English plans for the next day. The English would form up for a march in force on Stirling. They would not wait for the greater part of the English foot soldiers to wade across to join them. They would deploy the troops they had, get an early start and be in Stirling Castle in time for lunch.

Now King Robert had an option other than melting away into the night. He could take advantage of this intelligence in the morning and conduct a limited engagement with the English cavalry without the mass of Welsh footmen to interfere. Now the voices of the battle faction grew louder. The English are demoralised, they cried. If they struck again tomorrow, they could send half of them to their Maker and the rest of them packing back to England. The flight faction had no new argument. King Robert knew that if he failed to join battle in the morning, the commanders who were arguing for battle would take their men home.

Some time during the night a new piece of news was added to the equation. The Bruce's main supply train – withdrawn across Stirling Bridge to Cambuskenneth Abbey, for easy evacuation should the Scottish army need to flee – had been attacked and taken by the Earl of Atholl. On one hand, this loss was disappointing and demoralising to the Bruce. On the other, it made the decision to flee a bit more difficult, as the supplies they would need for their flight were now gone.

Ten years of painful education in guerrilla warfare had taught Robert not to join battle. Ten years of politicking had taught Robert that every ally was precious. Ten years of skulking in the bogs and mountains had whetted Robert's hunger for his kingdom. Ten years of waiting had taught him patience. Now, when sober consideration would appear to his allies as indecision, he needed to make a choice. He chose battle.

At sunrise, after the special mass for the feast of St John the Baptist, the Bruce's army would attack the English on their flank, and send the Plantagenet fleeing across the Bannockburn to ignominy in England. Then Stirling Castle could be dismantled, as it should have been the June before. Should the battle go against them, they would melt back into the woods where the English could not follow, and repair to Lennox until the Bruce was strong again.

The decision made, the council broke up and the commanders went to tell their men. Now King Robert could lay his head down, knowing that when next he slept it might be as a prisoner of the English, doomed to painful death as the traitor Earl of Carrick; perhaps as the long-time commander of a fugitive army spending one more night in the forest, king of Scotland only to his friends; or maybe as the victor over the Plantagenet, king of Scotland not only to his friends but also to his enemies.

The Scottish soldiers slept, knowing that when next they laid their heads down it would either be as living men or as corpses.

9

Stirling Carse

The way the English king disposed his troops on the morning of 24 June is by no means certain. We have a few sketchy descriptions. We have an idea of how Edward's father and Edward's own generals deployed in other battles. Further, we can deduce from the course of the battle and the lie of the land how and where the soldiers must have been standing when it began.

The many historians of the battle have all advanced their theories on the deployment of King Edward's troops into line of battle. Once again, these theories are based on the assumption that Edward did not know what he was doing. The chain of reasoning is as follows. The English were positioned to face the Scots (in order to conduct a battle). Archdeacon Barbour tells us that the English were all together in a mass of troops, so the battalions were all close together, facing the Scots. Generally this formation is drawn as a line of battle facing westward, either three battalions wide by three deep or four wide and two deep, with the king's battalion behind. We know that the vanguard charged first, so the vanguard is generally drawn as a separate battalion in front of (west of) the greater mass of English horsemen. We know that there were English archers ahead of and behind the knights when they faced westwards, towards the Scots and the Roman road, so a skirmishing line of archers is drawn ahead of (west of) the English vanguard, and another line behind. There is no mention at all of the Welsh knifemen and the English billmen being deployed or even involved in the battle. Sometimes they are drawn as part of the rear line of archers, and sometimes they are ignored.

The result is strikingly dissimilar to what we know about the way the English deployed. In the Welsh Wars, Edward Longshanks's generals learned to deploy their horse in line abreast (like a scrimmage in American football), with archers alternating with the horse or on the wings. This formation was learned from lessons like the Battle of Falkirk, when the English horse could not break Sir William Wallace's schiltrons with cavalry charges, and instead massacred Wallace's foot soldiers with archers. With their archers on their wings, an English army could shoot arrows until the enemy broke formation. Then the heavy horsemen could charge and further disperse them. This further 'dispersal' would, of course, involve a great deal of killing as well.

The result of Edward's deployment on the carse was that archers blocked horsemen, horsemen blocked other horsemen and everyone blocked the rest of the archers. Why, one might ask, did King Edward arrange his troops in this strange formation, with each arm blocking the next? Why, because he was a raving idiot, of course. Once it is assumed that the king of England was bungling the battle (which is an easy assumption, given the benefits of hindsight), we need not assume that his deployment was rational, and any deployment is possible.

If we abandon once again the idea that King Edward expected to fight a battle facing westward, we may also abandon the assumption that King Edward was an idiot, and all his generals with him. We start with the basic assumption that King Edward had come to Scotland to make a great show of force in relieving Stirling as well as to destroy the rebel Earl of Carrick. We proceed with the necessity of camping on the carse, as noted previously. We recall the formation of a central body of horse with archers on the wings. The result of this assumption and recollection is somewhat different from the traditional view of the pattern of English deployment at Bannockburn.

In re-drawing the pattern, we must first discard the dispositions of the individual battalions. These are generally drawn in some neat grid formation of slashed squares (the traditional symbol for troops of cavalry). Each historian has set out that grid to fit the piece of land he has chosen as the likeliest site for the battle, and most of these historians seem to assume that the commanders of the English battalions at Bannockburn had their battalions dressed in even squadrons, as though prepared to charge beneath Causeway Heights at Balaclava. While they could conceivably have been drawn up in precise squares, we have no evidence that orderly dressing was a military virtue in the fourteenth century. In the absence of evidence to the contrary, it can be ventured that the main force was not neatly ranked, or even delineated one battalion from the next. The men of each battalion needed only to keep track of their banneret's flag. Per usual Edwardian formation, the battalions were in rough line abreast, with a centre group and wing groups of cavalry, and the archers beyond the cavalry wings.

Now that we start with the expectation that an Edwardian army would wake up in the morning and form up like an Edwardian army, we are faced with a question. Why is it that Barbour says the Scots faced an army 'all in [one] schiltron', entirely different in shape from the one just described? The answer is that the Scots were seeing it from a different perspective: the flank.

In order to assume that the English formed their line facing westward, one must assume that the English expected a Scottish attack from the west, and were preparing to counter it. There is, however, no evidence that the English expected an attack. As we have seen, the Scots themselves had not expected to attack. They were a guerrilla army, not a field army. Open-field warfare was not their idiom. So there is no reason to assume that the English formed up facing westward.

If we assume instead that King Edward wanted to march on Stirling and afterwards use the castle as a base for infantry operations against the Bruce, a different picture is painted. He formed his army in a line facing north, towards Stirling (north-northwest, actually). Their road would be the broad, dry upper carse, and in the unlikely event that the Bruce put Keith's horse or even the whole army of infantry between him and the castle (not that it seemed likely), Edward would be prepared. Even if he admitted the possibility of a daylight engagement on the field, King Edward just hadn't expected an attack from the flank.

From the Scots' point of view, looking down on the side of the English line, the English looked to be formed all in one mass: one massive column. It was this end-on view that the Scottish soldiers saw as they came down the hill, and it was with the end of their line that the Earls of Gloucester and Hereford led the mighty counterattack of the English knights on the morning of St John's Day.

Stirling Carse
The Feast of the Nativity of St John the Baptist
Monday morning, 24 June 1314

English earls had in the past displayed a reluctance to wake up early on the morning of a battle. Even so, it is a good bet that Gilbert de Clare, Earl of Gloucester, did not sleep in. His ears still ringing from the abuse he had received at the king's table the previous night on account of suggesting a day of rest, he must have been awake early and kicking Sir Giles de Argentine out of bed and sending his servants to waken the Earl of Hereford. To any complaints that the sun had barely risen, and that they had got to sleep only a few hours before, Gloucester must have had a few choice words of reply. He was, after all, constable of the army, whatever Hereford had to say.

He wore a coat and leggings of tough cloth, though they might have been of tough raw silk embroidered with finer stuff, and over that a quilted jack less in preparation for battle than in protection against the damp morning chill. On his head he wore a woollen hood and on his feet stout leather shoes with a line of embroidery running from the pointed toe to the ankle. His squires were dressed in older or less expensive versions of the same clothing as they fed and warmed up the earl's charger, taking it down to the ford for a drink. Similar scenes were enacted many times over as the constable's men sent drummers throughout the camp to wake the soldiers and be pelted with garbage for their pains. Although the knights and their squires and men-at-arms could look forward to an exciting day of martial marching, and perhaps a bit of fighting and ransoming as well, nobody likes to wake up to the booming of a drum. Less so if the wine has been flowing in knightly quantities in anticipation of the re-supply at Stirling, and still less so if sleep had been less than peaceful, with constant dread of Scottish attack. Those who had been up all the chilly night, in armour and awaiting attack, with sniffles that would not go away, after long days on the road, were the ones who least welcomed the drummers, or any human company for that matter.

The priests, if not the bishops, had been up before dawn to pray, and had only napped until now. The camp awakening, they set about preparing for the mass that would celebrate the feast of the Nativity of St John the Baptist.

The footmen across the burn were harder to awaken if, indeed, anybody bothered to try. They did not have the same anticipation of the day's parade as did the knights. For them it would be just another day of hurry up and wait, and the provisions would be just as meagre and just as late at Stirling as they had been since their lords had mustered them weeks ago. It was easy on a chill June morning, with the mists lying low on the bog, to roll over in a nice woolly mantle and go back to sleep. If any of them expected more fighting that morning, so much more the reason for catching a few more winks. If there were a battle, a man could always wake up then, and make it to the field in time for the looting.

The horses were all particularly nervous. With an entire army of chargers, palfreys, pack-horses and oxen competing for a limited amount of meadow grass, there cannot have been enough to satisfy any of them. The horses of the important people – the king, the earls, the barons and some of the knights – had rich meal for fodder, and that without adequate straw to wash it down (inadequate by modern standards: remember that they appreciated a skittish stallion). As a result, some horses were nervous because they were underfed, and some were nervous because they were too richly fed. Many, like their riders, were additionally nervous from lack of sleep, having spent the night loosely saddled and bridled in anticipation of attack.

Yesterday's bread soaked in yesterday's wine served to break fast (there was likely no cold meat, since the previous day was a fast, the vigil of St John). The tents were struck, and the kitchens, and the wagons loaded to follow the army to Stirling.

The army formed up on an open field, the dry ground that sloped down to the bogs on the right and up to the woods on the left. Their objective was Stirling Castle, and their formation faced that fort, quite visible above the trees on its high rock across the carse. The ten battalions of horse were arranged with the marching vanguard as the left wing, the rear guard on the right. The king's battalion quite possibly led, in front of the line, and the battalions which formed the main body of their marching formation formed the main body of the army. In order to allow them a clear field of fire ahead, the archers were deployed on the wings, one group to the left of the vanguard and the other to the right of the king's battalion. Thus, if the Scots deployed between the English army and the castle, the archers could fill their schiltrons with arrows, just as the English archers and their Gascon comrades had done at Falkirk.

The soldiers all along the lines cast apprehensive glances at the forest atop the bluff. The smoke from the cook-fires was gone, and that probably meant that the Scots had gone. They were an army formed up in broad daylight to fight on a field, and Scottish armies didn't fight field armies. No, now that the sun was up they were safe from Scottish attack.

It was by no means easy for a constable and his staff to turn ten battalions of fiercely jealous noblemen and their stomping, snorting steeds, plus their squires and men-at-arms, into a functional line of battle. The task cannot have been made easier by the ongoing conflict as to precisely which of the two constables was actually in charge of the constabulary. No doubt the actual ordering of troops was conducted by knights who had done this sort of work before, and were able to bully and flatter the knights into formation regardless of which earl was theoretically in charge.

In each battalion each knight wanted to be in the front (except for those in whom the instinct for self-preservation overrode their desire for glory, ransom and booty). With no army facing them across the field, it seemed unlikely that there would be battle, and the cowards especially thought it a good day to muscle their way to the front, contributing to the disorder.

In the vanguard, the most prestigious battalion save the king's, there was especially keen competition once again. No doubt the constables and marshals had special difficulty getting these soldiers under control, with the Earl of Gloucester's men and the Earl of Hereford's men on the fiercest and heaviest-fed horses in the army jockeying for the best positions. Perhaps the Earl of Hereford needled the Earl of Gloucester, suggesting that he take a nap for a while, and perhaps the Earl of Gloucester spat and cursed and realised that in his haste to mount up and prove to his peers that he was no coward nor traitor, he had forgotten his surcoat. Well, no matter. It didn't look like rain, and without the surcoat everyone could admire his expensive imported armour.

The king was just deciding that the army was ready to move, and that with luck they could have lunch on a proper table in the castle, instead of on these damned camp tables among the flies. The horde of Welsh knifemen and second-class archers was just getting ready to wade the burn (resigning themselves to squishy shoes for the rest of the day). The drummers and trumpeters were just getting ready to make a great deal of noise by way of passing the order to advance, when a picket came thundering down the upper carse, waving his hat, but by the time his message was understandable, it was no longer important.

There, along the crest of the bluff, stood several hundred messengers, their sergeants' cries ringing out in the morning air. They stood along the ridge in a mob, covering it for a good part of its length. It was at first not clear what they were armed with; their spears' ash shafts blended in with the wood around, and the points were black from the forge. But this section of forest came down the bluff at the trot, in four rough groups, and stopped once the ground levelled off into the gentle field of the carse. There their front line knelt.

From far across the field, King Edward saw the forest of Scots' spears emerging from the wood. 'What!' he cried, perhaps accompanied with the sort of Anglo-Norman oath that clerical chroniclers prefer not to record. 'Will yonder Scots fight?' And incredulous he was, for his first impression was that they had come out to kneel in mass surrender. The unexpected had happened. The Scots were coming out to fight on an open field in broad daylight. It was Bruce's objective to keep Edward away from Stirling and send the Plantagenet home in disgrace. It was Edward's objective to crush the Bruce and his army. Although the English could have ridden for Stirling and made it ahead of the footbound Scots, they were bound by Edward's agenda to stop and fight. Edward was surprised, and pleased.

Remembering the durable Scottish formation from the previous day's fighting, Ingraham de Umfraville suggested that the English withdraw behind their baggage train, and that when the Scots broke formation to loot, the English could then descend upon them. Edward would have none of it. After all, if suggesting a day of rest marked the Earl of Gloucester as a coward, imagine what Giles de Argentine would say about a king withdrawing behind his baggage train. The trumpets sounded to make the army ready.

It took no orders to turn every English knight to his left. Every man's left hand pulled hard on the reins and turned his horse to face the new threat, though the beasts snorted and reared and spat. The earls in the vanguard pushed their way to the new front, the westward side of their battalion. The archers who now stood between the English van and the milling Scots needed no orders to begin shuffling aside. In the event, no orders came.

The New Park
The Feast of the Nativity of St John the Baptist
Monday morning, 24 June 1314

The dawn did not awaken the Scots as early as it did the English, shaded as the Scots were by the canopy of the forest.

It was less of a labour to wake their army as well. It had grown darker earlier in the wood, and in their sheltered position there they slept a good night, veterans of guerrilla war who knew that you took sleep when you could, regardless of the next day's agenda. They had formed their battalions before lying down, and they slept in their groups, their buddies nearby, so that there would be no chaotic milling in the morning.

The soldiers awoke. Each battalion heard mass, with the light of morning slanting through the leaves and the mists, then broke fast on yesterday's cold oat-cakes – there was no time to blow up banked embers to cook fresh breakfast.

With all the knights attending, King Robert knighted young Walter Stewart, and made the Black Douglas (the actual commander of Stewart's battalion) a knight banneret. Squires who were due the accolade were knighted, and those knights who would command others had the points torn off their pennons to make little square banners, 'bannerets', for recognition.

They assembled in their groups. They could all see the bright glow that was the edge of the forest, and they knew that on the other side of the tree line was death for some and wealth for others. They heard the jingling of harness as Keith the Marshal took his troop of horsemen up the road to St Ninian's Kirk. Their twofold purpose was to slow or stop the English should they try to run for Stirling, and to scatter any English archers who menaced the schiltrons.

Each man found his buddies and they stood, in their groups of tens and hundreds, waiting for the order to leave the trees. They held their pikes just behind the iron heads, with the long shafts trailing behind (to keep the points from catching in the branches above or sticking into their friends). Then the order came, shouted from Bruce's battalion or sounded on a horn, and the soldiers, careful not to tread on their comrades' pikes, walked out of the woods and into the morning of St John's Day.

They trotted down the bluff, each man keeping his buddy in sight, pikes straight up in the air now. They laughed at the sight of the English picquet, who had sheltered in the shadows of the bluffs all night, riding madly across the field, waving his hat before him and his buttocks behind. Seen end on, across the field, the English army was one deep mass, the various battalions of horse and archers indistinguishable. The sergeants shouted for them to stop once they had covered several yards of the level ground. There they formed their schiltrons.

King Robert placed three schiltrons in a line, which allowed him to block off a wide stretch of the carse and stand between the English and Stirling. Behind was his own schiltron, ready to fill any hole caused by two of the front-line schiltrons drifting apart. If there was no need for him to do that, he could throw his schiltron into the fray at some point when a strong push would be to his advantage.

Each group of friends formed its section of the wall. Perhaps they put their left hands on their buddies' shoulders, their right still holding their spears aloft. Sergeants began pushing outward, until the schiltrons took the shape of rough ovals. The reserve men stood within the oval, ready to be thrown by the sergeants into gaps left by dead men. Once the great hedgehogs of spears were deployed, and the outer rings had knelt to rest and to present a stable fence against cavalry, the orders ceased to be shouted and the soldiers subsided into a nervous silence, interrupted here and there by clansmen singing some family song and by priests chanting a hymn.

The concept of wheeling a line was unknown to European cavalry of the fourteenth century. There was no single order Edward could give that would cause the entire army to pivot on its left flank to face the Scots. If there had been such a command, there was no chance of executing it. The English line had been carefully marshalled, and once it began to move there was no restoring order. There was only one order to give European heavy cavalry, and that was to charge. A charge could be modified – it could curve to the left or to the right –however it could not stop once it had begun until it either hit an obstacle, like another army, or petered out piecemeal.

Just as the vanguard had charged on the first day of the battle, without any orders from Edward, so it charged today. Gilbert de Clare, Earl of Gloucester, was constable of the army, and by God and Saint George he would lead the charge. Humphrey de Bohun, Earl of Hereford, was constable of England, and his family would never be second. With a roar of battle-cries, the Earl of Gloucester and the Earl of Hereford and their retinues knocked their visors over their faces, put their spurs to their horses' flanks, and began to trot up the gentle slope towards the schiltrons. The Earl of Gloucester cocked his arm up to his armpit, the shaft of his lance hugged tightly under his arm. He locked his knees, pushing his feet hard into his stirrups, and he brought the top of his shield up close to his face. Beside him the Earl of Hereford did the same, and behind them their followers and friends did likewise. As the horses rumbled across the hard ground, Gloucester and his men gained on Hereford, and Gilbert de Clare was the first in the vanguard.

The horses were now the prime movers of the battle, not their riders. The chargers were skittish from rich food and poor sleep. They were also most of them stallions, and as they began to trot up the gentle slope their ancient herd instincts, old before the first cavalryman had tamed a wild horse, took over. Each stallion wanted to be ahead of the others. Each wanted to lead, just as the master of each wanted glory. The presence of even a few mares ridden by squires and men-at-arms exacerbated this fierceness. Their natural inclination to run up a slope sped the horses up, going from walk to trot to canter to hand-gallop to a thundering gallop that even the riders with their vicious spurs and curb bits could not control. They knew that if they tried too hard to stop their horses, leaning back in the saddle and pulling back with all their strength, the horses would sit down on their rumps, braced on their front legs, and the horses behind would fall over them, with great potential for injury. The horses thundered up the carse, towards the Earl of Carrick's battalion, while the knights shouted their war cries and anticipated the moment when the Scots would break and flee and be ridden down like dogs.

The moment never came. The Scots did not move. Their outer ring squatted on the ground, their spears butted to the ground, their sharp points in the air at about the height of a horse's neck or head (and the rider's abdomen). The inner rings held their spears with their points at the level of the horses' chests. They prayed or swore silently as the ground beneath them rumbled, the great steel juggernaut looming closer every second. The first English horses came to point of pike, and the pikemen closed their eyes tight.

A horse will not try to run down an obstacle. It will instead attempt to avoid it, or jump over it if it can. However, the perceived obstacle of the schiltron, dead ahead of Gloucester's horses, was still a pike's length away (some fifteen feet), when the first horse was speared. It might have been trying to slow or turn by that point, seeing and ranging the men (but not the slim pike-heads). Its rider might have been hauling back hard on the reins, trying desperately to stop once he saw that the Scots would not run. For the first horses, it was of no avail.

When the Earl of Gloucester and his friends hit the spears, their horses reared and plunged and turned, screaming in pain. Hereford's men and the rest of the vanguard were suddenly blocked by a wall of horseflesh, but carried onward by momentum to crash into Gloucester's men, sending them reeling into the range of the pikes. The horses on the flanks sheered off, trying to avoid the obstacle, and the horses of the later ranks tried to turn to get away from the pain and confusion.

The first line of the schiltron, the outer ring, held their pikes steady as the weight of horses broke them, or dropped them as horses fell on them. The men of the inner rings handed new spears outward. In turn, the men of the inner rings of the schiltrons took spears from the men in the centre, for they too had targets now. As the Gloucester horses were pushed into range by the following horses, the spearmen set the iron blades of their spears against trappers and horse-padding and against the joints of armour plate, and pushed hard, thrusting the points into the horses and, more importantly, into the riders. A wounded horse with a dead rider was an active obstacle to the English horsemen, obstructing and frightening the oncoming horses. The young man with the expensive, imported armour in the front of the

English line was a good target: he couldn't be worth ransoming or he would be wearing a surcoat with well-known arms. So Gilbert de Clare, Earl of Gloucester and Hertford, was cut down out of hand.

The sound of battle is a curious thing. While the English charged, they whooped their war-cries and shouted defiance at their enemies. The noises were hoof-beats and the voices of men. After the initial meeting of horses and spears, when the soldiers of both sides settled down to killing, the sound changed. Nobody had leisure to speak or sing, and the result was an eerie rumble of equipment and hooves. Armour clattered on armour and weapons thumped and scraped horses and men. The noise of battle was punctuated by the screams of horses and wounded men, and the occasional shout of an order.

The first shock of the charge was absorbed largely by the English front ranks, sending them reeling to their deaths. The vanguard piled up like a high-speed motorway accident, with the horses crashing into the ones before. Unlike cars in a motorway accident, horses do not eventually grind to a halt, and these fierce, powerful stallions turned and tried to flee. Some tried to flee through the following ranks, sowing discord and confusion. Others fled to one side or the other, some coming within spear range of the other schiltrons, others driven by their riders around the schiltrons, looking for a weak point to attack.

Once the following ranks of English horse had stopped pressing the leaders into spear range, there was nobody left for the pikemen to kill. Now the Earl of Moray gave orders that the outer rings of his battalion should rise from their knees. The Black Douglas, commanding the steward's battalion, and Edward Bruce, Earl of Carrick, soon followed suit. Once an entire schiltron was standing, the order came to advance towards the milling chaos of the English vanguard.

Sergeants on the leading side, the side which faced the English, began pushing their men forward. Sergeants on the trailing side began pulling their men, keeping the general oval shape of the schiltron. Now enemy horsemen were coming within range once again, and as they did they were stabbed at with the spears. Here and there a bolder spearman ran forward a few paces and, still within the hedge of pikes, stabbed at a target before being overtaken by his comrades' march forward. Their horses continued to try to flee. Those which succeeded in fleeing caused control problems further back in the English army. Men and horses on the ground presented a problem since horses do not like to tread on other horses or on people. This caused them to balk, although they could be urged and pushed into trampling man and beast with their cleated iron horseshoes.

The English cavalry continued to push forward, the men all along the line pressing towards the promise of glory and ransom. Those horses which were controlled by their masters and turned to face the Scots had no clear ground on which to gain momentum to use their lances, and could not get close enough to use their swords. If a knight ventured close enough to swing a sword at a pike, the flexible ash shaft would like as not bounce out of his way, cut and weakened but unbroken, while another pike stabbed towards his vitals or his horse. If a knight's stubborn refusal to give way held up a section of pikes, the neighbouring sections advanced around him, surrounding him on three sides so that he could not defend himself.

The English army pressed forward. If an unhorsed knight managed to make his way past the points of the pikes to menace the spearmen with his sword, men with axes would step out among the spears and attack, supported by pikes and some of the Ettrick archers who stood within the hedgehogs. It would take a great swordsman indeed to hack through several determined men with axes, while spear-points stabbed at his throat and abdomen, and while archers shot from point-blank range. If he did manage to muscle past the outer rings of the schiltron, however, he would only find himself facing many determined sergeants and men with axes and swords, quite capable of hacking armour and flesh to bits at their leisure, and his mail and plate did him little good here. Unless a horde of men followed this knight through the gap, it would close, and like an amoeba the schiltron would digest the intruder.

The English horsemen pressed forward. Cavalrymen who were merely unhorsed were trampled first by their own horses and men, and next by the advancing soldiers of the schiltrons. Once the outer rings had passed over an injured man, and if he surrendered, the men inside the ring decided by his surcoat and his equipment whether he was worth capturing for ransom. If he was, he was held securely within the schiltron. If the prisoner was not worth the trouble, then he was hacked to death with an axe.

The English horsemen pressed forward. The knights at the back of the army, who had been on the right flank when the army had formed up in the morning, could not see what was happening in the mêlée ahead. They could only hear the sounds of battle, and knew that they wanted to be in it. So long as the battalions of mounted knights continued to ride towards their enemies, as they had been trained to do since they were boys, the knights who were close against the schiltrons could not flee or even gain room to fight. So long as the press of horses led only to the points of sharp Scottish spears, the English knights continued to be unhorsed, disabled and killed, without room to swing a sword.

The knights on the flanks were the ones who could escape, both to harry the flanking schiltrons and to turn back with the news. Stop the pushing, they cried. Hold fast, but do not charge. Pull back and make room to fight. Arrows from the Ettrick men clattered off their armour and equipment and tangled in their horses' trappers. Some struck home, especially among the lighter-armoured squires and other men-at-arms. None of the English cavalry was trained to listen to them.

The English archers who had been deployed on the army's left had had to flee to one side (the north, towards the castle), in order to avoid being ridden down by the English vanguard. Others might have been deployed between the English vanguard, on their left wing, and the English centre. This second group of archers, and any archers who had been deployed on the right of the broad English army, were blocked by their own men from shooting at the Scots. The first group, however, had a clear field of fire against the Scottish left flank. Given their leisure to shoot, the English archers could turn the battle into another Falkirk, where archers slaughtered standing Scottish schiltrons.

Now Robert Keith, marshal of Scotland, offered a demonstration of the use of cavalry against foot soldiers. Just as the English had ridden hard at the schiltrons, expecting the infantry to flee in terror of the great beasts and their armed and armoured riders, so the Scots expected the same thing. Keith and his troop, watching from St Ninian's Kirk, saw the English archers coming to some order and shooting. Keith shouted a battle-cry and knocked shut the visor of his helmet.

Keith's men thundered across the carse, lances fixed, shields up and heads down. Those archers who did not see their approach, or hear it over the noise of the battle, were alerted by the screams of their friends. Perhaps some of them bothered to shoot some arrows at the oncoming horses. Perhaps some of the arrows did not bounce off the shields, curved bascinets and breastplates or face guards. Some of those which struck home struck with enough force to injure the knights or the horses who were their targets. At bottom, however, any archers who stayed could shoot only from the time they first saw the horses (or from when the horses first came into range) until they lost their nerve (or were killed). That time, less than a minute, was not enough time to slow down Keith's horse. The archers ran from the horsemen, and the ones who did not scatter quickly enough went from being soldiers to being casualties, spitted on light lances, slashed with swords or clubbed with maces as the horses thundered past. Once the only successful cavalry action of the battle was complete, the Scottish horsemen fled the field, lest a group of English knights engage them. Their job was done.

The remaining English archers – those who were positioned on the English right flank – could not get a clear shot at the schiltrons. Their own cavalry were in the way, blocking their view, and with the English horse and the Scottish foot soldiers pressing so close together, shooting their arrows high into the air would endanger both sides equally. It is not likely, for that matter, that a high-angle shot, with little opportunity to aim, would be effective against the schiltrons. Dropping arrows would tend to be deflected by helmets and, since a schiltron is mostly empty space, they would also tend to fall into the empty ground inside the walls of the formation. Some shot anyway, and just as likely brought their own men down as any Scots.

It does not seem that the main body of English cavalry actually engaged the schiltrons, whether they charged at all or whether they stood still and allowed the Scots to push their way towards them. Had they decided to charge, archers who had fled from Keith were standing in the way. It would have been the third time they were ridden down: first by their own charging vanguard, second by Keith's light horse, and now by their own main body of cavalry.

The morning high tide, coming in at about eleven, was turning the Polls into something less comfortable than a bit of boggy ground. The soft, wet, salt marsh might have been passable to a horse carefully picking its way around obstacles and sink holes, but to ride across it in numbers and at speed was quite dangerous. The Bannockburn's course behind the army ran through a gully, where the stream raced through a series of deep meanders. These features now closed the English in to the north-east and east. The Scottish army stood to the west. Escape could thus only be northwards to Stirling, or southwards, across the ford.

The Scots army advanced, killing and forcing knights to choose between flight and death. Some of the English knights began to realise that the battle was going against them. If the Scots continued to advance, the English would be pushed back against the gully where they would have no chance at all of running their chargers up to speed. Then they would be defenceless against the great spiny hedgehogs that menaced and killed their comrades. They might have tried to run north, cross the Pelstream, there to re-form and attack again. They might have been outright unknightly and made an orderly withdrawal across the ford. They might even have dismounted and counterattacked with their lances. All of these, however, are suggested with the benefit of hindsight. None of these options were in the vocabulary of the knights. Their tactic was to charge. Footmen would run away, and horsemen would charge back with a great breaking of lances and bones. If horsemen ran away they were cowards, and if footmen charged back... well that just didn't happen. It is doubtful that many of the knights, except those in the killing zone, realised what was going on at all. Many of them continued to press forward, thinking that there was productive fighting going on ahead, and that they could help and gain by pitching in.

King Robert had known that King Edward would engage him, since that had been the Plantagenet's purpose in coming north. However, once the English were put in a position of disadvantage, Robert had no way of knowing whether they would remain engaged or whether they would run for Stirling. There the English could rest, to begin the fighting anew on more advantageous ground. King Robert much preferred the English to flee in disorder, through the scorched earth of Peebles and Lothian, to England. Now the Bruce took action to ensure this, bringing his own battalion into play. From their reserve position, behind the main body of the army, his men jogged around the leftmost schiltron, keeping track of their buddies as they went, then stopped. Just ahead and to the left of the other schiltrons, King Robert's battalion formed their oval and bristled their pikes outwards. Now the Scottish line consisted of three schiltrons in a row, with a fourth cupping around the north-west side of the English army and finally cutting it off from Stirling Castle.

The English were closed in by the Burn, by the Polls and by the Scottish army. There was now no mistaking the backward progress of their people, and the steady advancement of their enemies. It soon became apparent that something was dreadfully wrong. No orders issued from King Edward, however, and direction would have to come from elsewhere.

On the slopes of Coxet Hill the remains of King Robert's baggage train waited, packed and ready to flee, should the battle go against the Scots. The camp followers and victuallers watched from trees and clearings as the Bruce's schiltron swung into action, and from one of the two clear views of the battle (Stirling Castle also had a clear picture of what was going on) they saw that the Scots army was going to win. They cheered among themselves, and congratulated each other. Each pointed out his own contribution to the war effort. One fellow had polished the Bruce's helmet, another had sewn new soles to the Earl of Moray's boots, a third had sharpened the Black Douglas's sword. It took a little while for the logical consequence of victory to occur to them. The men on the field would get the loot. The men on the hill would get nothing.

One man from among the 'small folk' on the hill suggested that they form their own battalion and pitch in on the battlefield. This would give them the same right of plunder as the real soldiers. The others agreed and appointed the first man as their captain. A sheet of cloth from the launderers was hoisted on a pole by way of a banner, and taking their axes and hammers and pointed sticks they ran down the hill and through the park. When they issued from the trees of the New Park their captain rallied them around their banner and cried a charge down the bluff.

The English, just now becoming aware that the battle was going against them, now had a frightening sight to behold. There, where first three, then four Scottish battalions had stood, there came a fifth, banners flying amid whooping and screaming as they ran down the hill.

Once it became clear that there was no longer room for the Plantagenet horse to rally and charge again, the Earl of Pembroke and Sir Giles de Argentine, who had been detailed to hold their king's reins, decided that it was time for King Edward to leave. They and a guard led King Edward, protesting that he wanted to mix it in too, across the Polls and the Pelstream. The leopards of Anjou were seen leaving the field just as the new Scottish battalion was charging down the hill.

Now the English chivalry and their men-at-arms, as well as the English and Welsh foot soldiers, realised that if they stayed to fight they would be captured or killed. Those who were not bothered by this stayed, hopelessly battering at the schiltrons. Giles de Argentine was one of these. From the rear, where he had stood with his king, he had little idea of what happened to the Earl of Gloucester and his men. All he knew was that a pack of penurious peasants were pushing and panicking a line of English knights. As soon as he and the Earl of Pembroke had brought King Edward out of the fray, with a clear run to Stirling, he turned his horse towards the Scots, across the clear ground between the carse and Stirling, and put in his spurs. His battle cry of 'de Argentine! de

Argentine!' rang in his helmet, but was little heard elsewhere as his horse gathered speed. The charger was nervous and skittish, as the Earl of Gloucester's had been, but it did not have the herd instinct and a gentle uphill slope to speed it up and out of control. It was at a hand gallop that Sir Giles, the third greatest knight in all of Christendom, realised that the Scots were not going to break. It was just as his horse was preparing to jump the men twelve feet away that Giles de Argentine realised that death wasn't something that only happened to other people. The horse had not even begun to leap when its armour was struck by spear-points. As it stumbled and twisted its way to the ground, more spears struck Sir Giles de Argentine, and those or the deadly axes killed him.

Most of the knights turned their horses towards the ford, the gully or the Polls and rode hard. Of the men who tried to flee across the Polls, some made it to Stirling Castle, but many were mired or injured in the bog there, and drowned when the tide came in. Of the men who tried to charge down the gully and across the deep cut of the burn, some made it across, to ride upstream in search of a bank shallow enough to scale. Many, however, fell from stumbling horses and into the deep, fast waters of the burn to drown. Most made for the same ford they had crossed at the previous day. The Welsh foot soldiers, who had ventured across in hopes of looting the dead, now found themselves desperately trying to cross back. Complicating their crossing were several hundred big men on horses, thundering down the bank with little care for the infantrymen below.

Once the English had turned tail, there was no longer a need to maintain the tight schiltron formation. All the spears could be pointed forward now, and the reserves from the centres of the ovals could hardly be held back from helping out. The spears pushed forward, aided more often now by men with axes. The English retreat turned into a panic, and the ford at the Bannockburn was a killing ground, knights killing each other and their own infantry in their desperation to ride across the burn. Some of the Scots put down their spears when they got to the baggage trains of the English knights, but enough men remained on the attack to keep the pressure on the English.

Once resistance had ceased completely, and the Scots had to run to keep up with the English retreat, most of the army stopped chasing and killing, and turned to start looting. The priests among the Bruce's men wiped the blood from their axes and blessed themselves, thanking St John the Baptist for his support on this, his feastday. Cheers rose from the Scottish army as brothers and sons and clansmen found each other in the confusion and celebrated not being dead. The adrenaline of battle, the blood lust, the relief of being alive and finding kin and the greed of looting turned the army into a huge party. A great whooping roar rose from the Scottish soldiers and, as they ran, the English who fled looked over their shoulders to see a man in a crown being held aloft on the shoulders of Scottish earls and knights. The Battle of Bannockburn was ended.

10

The End

The king of England and his troop rode hard for Stirling
Castle: the nearest English garrison. Seeing the great red banner coming, Sir Philip de Mowbray, the governor, cried to his
porters to shut the gates. The king of England raged beneath
the walls. It was his castle, by God, and he had relieved it in
time. Whose side was Mowbray on, anyhow? Mowbray
replied that, although the bargain he had struck with Edward
Bruce was concluded in the English favour by the arrival of
the Plantagenet army near the fortress, that morning's battle
made the castle's fate less clear. If the English wished to hold
Stirling, they would need to go through the long process of
siege, and without the shipborne supplies they had been
expecting from Edinburgh. That was hardly a proper place for
the English king, bottled up in a fortress in Scotland while his
barons plotted against him at home. Mowbray kept the king
out for his own good.

The king of England turned his horse, and rode as quickly as he could around the forests towards safety. He rode for
Linlithgow, pursued by a small force under the eager Black
Douglas. The Black Douglas did not have the numbers to
overhaul and fight the English king's troop, but he dogged
their steps as long as he could, killing or capturing stragglers

and any knights who stopped to relieve themselves along the road.

Some historians of Bannockburn have lamented that King Robert did not have heavy cavalry on hand to dash around the English army to the east side, trap the army there and turn the rout into a massacre. This, of course, presumes that King Robert was interested in butchering a horde of English, Welsh and Scottish farmers and engaging in some hostage-taking with the English knights. This also ignores the fact that the Bruce's army was a guerrilla army that had one day on the field. Before Bannockburn and after, the Bruce had no use for heavy horse. Since he did not have a force of heavy cavalry to cut them off and allow his spearmen hours of gutting enjoyment, the point is moot.

A single steeplechase course being used simultaneously for horse and foot races might be comparable to the scene at the side of the Bannockburn. An additional thing to keep in mind, however, is that all the participants were armed, and in this situation one's rivals for crossing-space become one's enemies. Even at the best crossing-places the horse and foot soldiers fought to be the first across, with the Scots howling at their heels.

The English soldiers closest to the Pelstream could flee northward and through the Polls. Remember that while the army as a whole was cornered by the burns and bogs, the individual man on horseback or on foot could pick his way across unfriendly terrain. They made their way to the nearest safe place: the great rock that was the foundation of Stirling Castle. The gate was closed, but there was nowhere to go except back down the hill to the east, where the Scots were. Once King Robert felt secure on the carse he sent a force (likely Keith's light horsemen) to chase the refugees from the rock.

Once away, the survivors of the stream and the swamps and the spears could make their way south. Now, for the first time in weeks, they could make for a familiar place without the horrible dread of battle. With no useful maps to guide them cross-country, and no familiarity with manors other than their own, they must have followed the Roman road system that had brought them north. Sir Maurice de Barclay took command of the Welsh foot soldiers. Indeed, the system of constables needed to be maintained all the way back to each soldier's home manor, to keep the angry, hungry soldiery from travelling home like a swarm of locusts, denuding the English countryside as they went.

The Scots on the field began the work of looting. Every dead man had a purse, and every rich knight had a wagon. If a man was not quite dead, the situation could be easily rectified with an axe. Every Scottish soldier, from the king down, wanted a maximum share of the loot, and every soldier was armed. Now the Scottish constables saw to the orderly looting, seeing to it that the soldiers did not fall to blows over every purse and coin, and every piece of armour. The English baggage train was put under the command of Scottish royal officers, so that King Robert would be sure of his rightful share.

Only when the corpses were stripped of everything of value were they pitched into pits, or polls, or left for the local peasants to bury. Dead knights were returned to their families or not as the families could afford. The Earl of Gloucester was taken to a church to be watched over for the night, and then returned to his family in great state, at his cousin King Robert's personal expense.

Nobody tells us what Sir Marmaduke Thweng did during the battle, or how he came to be hiding under cover, with his armour stashed out of sight. As the afternoon wore on, this stalwart of the English side saw that trying to run for England was a chancy thing. He had seen the patrols of horse that the Bruce had sent after the Plantagenet, and he decided that he had a better chance by appealing to his old friend the Scottish king than by trying to outrace unfriendly patrols. He spent the night in hiding, while the Scots finished off the wounded and robbed the dead. He watched as they built their cook-fires and grilled their oat-cakes. They had an especially fine dinner, butchering the livestock brought along to feed the English earls and drinking the ale and wine from the English sumpter wagons that had been so well stocked at Edinburgh. He slept there, wrapped in his surcoat and gambeson, until morning, when he rolled up the armorial coat and went looking for King Robert.

The Bruce was glad to see his old friend. Who captured you, the Bruce asked. Thweng replied that he had not yet been put in the bag, and yielded himself to the Bruce. King Robert appreciated the gesture, and after guesting his defeated enemy for a while, sent him home with gifts and for no payment of ransom.

Conclusions

The first conclusion that may be drawn is that Bannockburn was a fight of the common man against the proud knight, in which the common man threw off the yoke of feudal oppression. This would be true if the ordinary pikeman of Stirling carse had been fighting for himself and his comrades. In fact, he was fighting for King Robert, whose rule came from his royal blood and his good right arm rather than from the Scots he was king of.

A second conclusion may be that Bannockburn was a fight of the Scots against the proud English, in which the downtrodden Scot threw off the yoke of English oppression and battled for Scotland's freedom. This would be true if Scotland had become an independent economy and polity and remained one for an appreciable length of time. Actually, though a Scottish culture flourished just as any people's folk culture flourishes, with its own music and literature, there was no independent Scottish polity or economy. The Highlands were a law unto themselves until the eighteenth century and the Borders were the same. A state called Scotland did indeed exist, with its own church and its own laws, but English hegemony was strong enough that the coronation of King Robert was not the birth of the nation, and the union of the crowns in 1603 was not the death of the nation. Scotland was a nation long before the victory at Bannockburn, and it has remained so long after King Robert's subsequent defeats, and the repeated defeats of his Stewart descendants.

A third conclusion that may be formed is that Bannockburn was a bloody event in a dynastic struggle for control of Scotland between the House of Plantagenet and the House of Bruce. The House of Bruce, headed by the king of Scotland, lasted for a generation, then died out. The crown of Scotland found its way through Robert's daughter to the descendants of young Walter Fitzalan the Steward, which descendants later married into the Tudors. Just as the Stewards gained their crown by female line, so the Tudors gained theirs by a combination of a female line and a bit of hard fighting (butchering any remaining Plantagenets along the way). When the Tudors finished their run, James Stewart was king of both England and Scotland, heir of both Edward Longshanks and Robert Bruce.

The Battle of Bannockburn determined the fates of a large number of men. Scores of men screamed their last breaths on the boggy carse on St John's Day. Hundreds of mothers and wives, on both sides of the border, mourned their men for years after. Edward Bruce and Philip Mowbray made a bargain, and blood soaked the marshes of Stirling. In the long term the achievement came to an historical footnote: a line in a few Scottish rants and English dirges.

War is currently viewed by many as an unpleasant aberration in human behaviour. Thus it is common among modern historians to eschew the study of war in favour of the study of more legitimate and pleasant activities. This does not do justice to the hundreds of Scotsmen, Englishmen and Welshmen who were taken to Stirling to fight, nor to the knights who took them there. Many were victims of their education and upbringing, many more were victims of a harsh social system. Many of them were not victims at all, emerging from the experience with loot and the thrill of victory for their pains. All were caught up in a complex web of interests and social behaviour which brought them to fight, and the story of their experience is as important as any other in history.

51 The falchion – 'a short, crude meat-cleaver of a sword'.

52 Military horseshoes, showing flanges and cleats, after the Luttrell Psalter.

Above: 53 Sir Roger de Trumpington, drawn from a brass dated 1280. Sir Roger's head rests on his 'heaume' or great helm, which is attached to his belt by a chain, allowing him to throw it off without losing it. His shield, painted with trumpets as a pun on his surname, hangs from his right shoulder on a gigue strap across his chest. The brass clearly shows the strap arrangement designed to hang his sword low on the left as he sits on his horse. His ailettes, also painted with the trumpets and crosses of his shield, are pushed back from his shoulders.

Above: 54 Mourning knights, Easter Sepulchre, Lincoln Cathedral. The knights are armed with mace, sword and shield.

Left: 55 Effigy of a knight, *c.*1310, Dorchester Abbey, Oxfordshire. The shield from this effigy has partially broken away, revealing clearly the shield's gigue strap and the drape of his surcote. The knight is depicted in the act of drawing his sword, most of which has also broken away.

56 A knight identified as A. Pembrugge, effigy, *c.*1320, Clehonger, Herefordshire. The knight is shown wearing his bascinet as well as wrought-iron protection for his shoulders, knees, shins and feet. Scalloped padding separates the mail coif from the armour beneath, and the knee cops from the shin guards. Disc-shaped plates protect the armpit and the inside of the elbow.

Clockwise from top:

57 A knight identified as Sir John de la Beche, effigy, *c.*1320, Aldworth, Berkshire. Sir John's knee armour is made from articulated pieces of iron suspended from the padding beneath his mail.

58 The jousting helm of Sir Richard Pembridge, KG, who died in 1375. This 'barrel helm' was made in three parts, the lower cylinder, the cone and the top section, which were then welded together. The metal thickens and turns outward to provide protection around the eyes.

59 Madoc ap Llewellyn ap Griffin, effigy, *c.*1331, Gresford, Denbigh. Madoc's effigy takes pains to fold back his surcote to show not only the hem of his knee-length mail but also the 'gamboised cuisses', padded breeches, beneath.

Left: 60 Sir William Staunton, 1326.
This carving at Staunton,
Nottinghamshire, shows the two most
recognisable features of an armoured
knight: his painted shield and his great
helm. Sir William's helmet is roughly
conical and does not appear to have a
visor. The ring at the top permits Sir
William to attach a decorative crest. It
is decorated with a flowery cross and
the air holes are also cut in a cross
pattern.

Opposite above: 61 Effigy, *c.*1320, Halton
Holgate, Lincolnshire. The knight is
shown wearing a bascinet over his mail
coif. The bascinet appears to have a
moveable visor, indicating that the
knight was accustomed to fighting
without his great helm. This effigy
shows wrought-iron plates covering
the knight's elbows and right wrist.

Below: 62 Sir Robert de Keynes, effigy,
1310, Dodford, Hampshire. Sir Robert
wears a bascinet over his mail coif as
well as hard cops to protect his elbows.

Right: 63 Sir Robert Shurland, drawn from an effigy at Minster, Kent. This sketch shows clearly the strap arrangement on the back of Sir Robert's shield, made visible by the loss of the figure's right arm.

Far right: 64 An English foot soldier wearing a padded jacket and iron cap and carrying a brown bill (after the Maciejowski Bible, *c.*1280). The knife at his belt is for use when eating and as a tool rather than for combat.

Top: 65 Armoured knights are interspersed with the evangelists on the Bruce cenotaph, fifteenth century.

Above: 66 The handle of the Hawthornden sword, one of the famous Scottish blades reputed to have been wielded by Robert the Bruce. The handle is made from a narwhal tusk and the guards are bent towards the blade to prevent the antagonist's sword from glancing off towards the wielder.

Right: 67 The huge two-handed sword, five feet nine inches in length and weighing seven and a half pounds, that some say was wielded by Sir Christopher Seton when he defended Robert the Bruce at Methven. The sword probably dates from the 1500s.

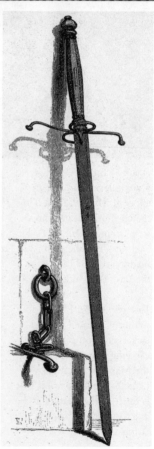

Above: 68 Combatants in a mounted mêlée, from the early-fourteenth-century manuscript known as Queen Mary's Psalter. The combatants are in mail and long surcoats and are fighting with sword and mace. Some wear their great helms with fan crests. While this kind of fully mounted combat featured only peripherally at Bannockburn, the weapons pictured were all in evidence.

Left (top): 69 This iron battle-axe head was found at Bannockburn. It is a purpose-built weapon for use against heavy armour rather than an axe from a peasant's tool shed.

Left (bottom): 70 Figure of a prior with a heraldic shield, Bruce cenotaph, fifteenth century. Just as with the English knights, the Scots relied on heraldic devices to distinguish each other in the field, and heraldry became an important part of life in war and peace.

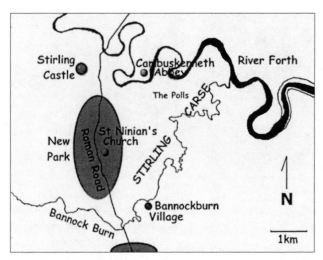

71 Stirling and Carse

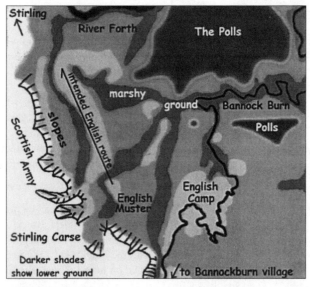

72 The English Plan

Clockwise from top left: 73, 74 The arms of Aylmer de Valence, Earl of Pembroke (left) and Sir Giles de Argentine, who rode on either side of Edward II.

75 The coat of arms of Gilbert de Clare, Earl of Gloucester, constable of the English army, who headed the vanguard during the march. Clare and Robert Bruce were first cousins.

76 The arms of Robert Clifford, at forty-one years old a veteran, who had been noted for his prowess under Edward I.

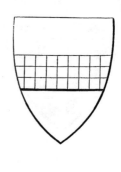

Clockwise from above left:

77 An English knight without his shield, coat of arms and great helm. The drawing represents Gilbert de Clare, Earl of Gloucester, who thus rode out on the second day of Bannockburn.

78 The arms of Walter the Steward, leader of a battalion at Bannockburn, who married Bruce's daughter and whose son later became King Robert II.

79 English knight in armour, late thirteenth century.

80 Carlisle, 1315. Initial letter of Edward II's charter to Carlisle in 1316. The Scots are shown attacking the city with a 'machine for casting stones', while a miner with a pick works at the foot of a wall.

81 Sir Geoffrey Luttrell, from the Luttrell Psalter, illuminated in 1340.

Bibliography

Medieval Documents

Rotuli Scotiae (The Scottish Rolls in the Tower of London), Public Record Office. This document consists of the file copies of all royal correspondence dealing with Scotland. I am indebted to Dr Jeffrey L. Singman of the Higgins Armoury Museum for his translations from the Latin.

All the English royal rolls of the period: the fine rolls, close rolls, charter rolls, chancery warrants etc., have titbits of interest to the student of the matter of Edward II's Stirling Campaign.

Statute of Winchester, 13 Edward I (1285). This document mandates military contributions from English noblemen by income and holdings. This statute was theoretically in force from the end of the thirteenth century until the first half of the sixteenth century.

Chronicle of Lanercost. Trans. Rt Hon. Sir Herbert Maxwell, Bt. Glasgow: James Maclehose and Sons, 1913. This chronicle was prepared by the monks of Lanercost, near Carlisle.

Baker, Geoffrey (fl. 1350). *Chronicon Galfridi le Baker de Swynebroke*. Edited with notes by Sir Edward Maunde Thompson. Oxford: Clarendon Press, 1889. The *Chronicle* of Geoffrey le Baker includes a biography of King Edward II, including his abdication and death.

Barbour, John, Archdeacon of Aberdeen (1316?-1395). *The Bruce*. Trans. George Eyre-Todd. London, Glasgow: Gowans and Gray, 1907. This is an heroic epic of the life of Robert Bruce prepared by a Scottish cleric in the late fourteenth century.

Capgrave, John (1393-1464). *The Chronicle of England*. Ed. F.C. Hingeston-Randolph. London: Longman, Brown, Green, Longmans and Roberts, 1858. Our weather report for Britain in 1314 comes from this chronicle, courtesy of Professor Lynn Nelson of the University of Kansas.

Gray, Sir Thomas of Heton (d. 1369?). *Scalacronica*. Trans. Rt Hon. Sir Herbert Maxwell of Monreith, Bt. Glasgow: James Maclehose and Sons, 1907. This is a chronicle prepared by a northern knight whose father fought and was captured at Bannockburn.

Secondary Sources

Barow, G.W.S. *Robert Bruce and the Community of the Realm of Scotland*. Edinburgh: Edinburgh University Press, 1976. This is the most complete scholarly analysis of Bruce's career, and of Bannockburn.

Becke, Maj. A.F., R.F.A. 'The Battle of Bannockburn' in G.E.C. Cokayne's *Complete Peerage*, vol. XI. London: St Catherine Press, 1949. This analysis of the battle owes a great deal to modern preconceptions and to later Scottish traditions.

Bingham, Caroline. *The Life and Times of Edward II*. London: Weidenfeld and Nicolson, 1973.

Bradbury, Jim. *The Medieval Archer*. New York: St Martin's Press, 1985. Bradbury gives the reader a fresh picture of the medieval archer and his military colleagues. It has an especially interesting chapter on Robin Hood.

Contamine, Philippe. *War in the Middle Ages*. Trans. Michael Jones. Oxford: Basil Blackwell, 1984.

Davis, R.H.C. *The Medieval Warhorse*. London: Thames and Hudson, 1989. This book is a splendid overview of the breeding and use of warhorses, especially in England.

Devries, Kelly. *Infantry Warfare in the Early Fourteenth Century: Discipline, Tactics, and Technology*. Woodbridge, Suffolk: Boydell Press, 1996. Dr DeVries's book has a chapter on Bannockburn, and while it suffered some harsh criticism on publication, it is one of the few good, current works on the subject.

Fenton, Alexander and Stell, Geoffrey (eds). 'Land Routes: The Medieval Evidence' in *Loads and Roads in Scotland and Beyond: Road Transport over 6000 Years*. Edinburgh: John Donald, 1984.

Bibliography

Miller, Reverend Thomas. 'The Site of the New Park in relation to the Battle of Bannockburn' in the *Scottish Historical Review*, vol. XII, no. 45 (October 1914).

Morris, John E. *Bannockburn*. Cambridge: Cambridge University Press, 1914. This book gives a clear description of the battle, and excellent photographs of Stirling carse before the subdivisions came.
—*The Welsh Wars of Edward I*. Oxford: Clarendon, 1901.

Scott, Ronald McNair. *Robert the Bruce, King of Scots*. London: Hutchinson, 1982.

Wormald, Jenny (gen.ed.). 'Kingship and Unity: Scotland 1000-1306' in *The New History of Scotland*. Toronto: University of Toronto Press, 1981.

List of Illustrations

schiltron. The Bruce Pictures Ltd.

44 Actors representing Scottish footsoldiers wear steel bascinets over mail coifs. The Bruce Pictures Ltd.

45 Actors representing Scottish pikemen kneel to receive the English cavalry charge. The Bruce Pictures Ltd.

46 A view of the battlefield from a position hovering over the Tor Wood. Cromwell Productions Ltd.

47 The triangle of the Bannockburn, the River Forth and the wooded high ground to the west of the road. Cromwell Productions Ltd.

48 A view from Skeoch, near Bannockburn village. Cromwell Productions Ltd.

49, 50 King Edward II's battle plan. Cromwell Productions Ltd.

51 The falchion. Sketch by the author.

52 Military horseshoes. Sketch by the author.

53 Sir Roger de Trumpington, drawn from a brass dated 1280. Tempus Archive.

54 Mourning knights, Easter Sepulchre, Lincoln Cathedral. Tempus Archive.

55 Effigy of a knight, *c.*1310, Dorchester Abbey. Tempus Archive.

56 A knight identified as A. Pembrugge, effigy, *c.*1320. Tempus Archive.

57 A knight identified as Sir John de la Beche, effigy, *c.*1320. Tempus Archive.

58 The jousting helm of Sir Richard Pembridge, KG. Tempus Archive.

59 Madoc ap Llewellyn ap Griffin, effigy, *c.*1331. Tempus Archive.

60 Sir William Staunton, 1326. Tempus Archive.

61 Effigy, c.1320, Halton Holgate, Lincolnshire. Tempus Archive.

62 Sir Robert de Keynes, effigy, 1310. Tempus Archive.

63 Sir Robert Shurland, drawn from an effigy at Minster, Kent. Tempus Archive.

64 An English foot soldier wearing a padded jacket and iron cap and carrying a brown bill. Sketch by the author.

65 Armoured knights are interspersed with the evangelists on the Bruce cenotaph, fifteenth century. Tempus Archive.

66 The handle of the Hawthornden sword. Tempus Archive.

67 A huge two-handed sword dating from the 1500s. Tempus Archive.

68 Combatants in a mounted mêlée, as depicted in Queen Mary's Psalter. Tempus Archive.

69 This iron battle-axe head was found at Bannockburn. Tempus Archive.

70 Figure of a prior with a heraldic shield. Tempus Archive.

71 Stirling and Carse. Sketch by the author.

Index

Index

Index

Patent Rolls 12
Pelstream 146, 179, 206, 208, 212
Picts 23
Plantagenet, Geoffrey, Count of Anjou
   and Maine 29
Plantagenet, House of 29, 32, 38, 49-50,
   215-216
Polls, The 139-140, 142, 146, 167-171,
   205, 207-209, 212-213
Pontefract, West Riding of Yorkshire 41
Ponthieu 32-33
Pope 50, 120

Queensferry (North or South) 25

Richard I, King of England 30, 152
road, Roman 86, 114, 138, 140-142,
   144-146, 159, 178, 180, 186, 213
Rome 31-32, 45, 49-50, 55
Roxburgh 10, 64

Scarborough, Castle 37, 109
schiltron 106, 132-138, 155, 159-163,
   173, 177, 180, 186, 188, 191, 195-197,
   199-209
Seton, Alexander 181
Seton, Christopher 44, 59, 222
Stirling Bridge 25, 53, 138, 169
Stirling Bridge, battle, 1297 53, 182
Stirling, castle 11, 25-28, 41, 54-55, 63,
   65, 67, 69, 114-115, 118, 145, 154-155,
   162, 170, 175-176, 178, 181-183, 187-
   188, 191, 194-196, 205-209, 211-212,
   224
Stirling, siege of, 1305 54-55, 57

Stirling, shire, town and carse 11, 14, 17,
   25, 53-56, 68, 87, 108, 112, 114, 138-
   139, 141-132, 144-146, 150, 159, 167,
   172, 176, 178, 190, 216, 224
sunrise and sunset 178-179

taxation 30-31, 40, 70, 72, 116
Templars, Knights 34, 119-120
Thweng, Marmaduke 19, 214
Tor Wood 65, 115-116, 118, 132, 137-
   139, 141, 149-150, 154, 159-160, 162,
   165, 169, 180, 234
Tynemouth 37

Ulster, Richard de Burgh, Earl of 10,
   59, 65, 119
Umfraville, Ingraham or Ingelram de
   19, 54-56, 81, 121, 194

Valence, Aylmer, Earl of Pembroke 37,
   58, 60-61, 109-110, 151, 155-156, 176,
   208, 225

Wales 24, 28, 30, 32, 42, 48, 67-68, 85,
   87, 108, 122, 128, 144, 175, 180
Wallace, William, of Lanark 25, 52-55,
   106, 133, 162, 178, 180, 186
Waltham 34
Wark-on-Tweed 69, 85-87, 108, 111-
   112, 114-115, 119, 150, 173
Warwick, Earl of 37

York, see of 48, 52, 63
York, city 42